THE
ACCIDENTAL
ADULT

THE ACCIDENTAL ADULT

Essays and Advice for the RELUCTANTLY RESPONSIBLE and MARGINALLY MATURE

COLIN SOKOLOWSKI

adamsmedia
Avon, Massachusetts

Published by
Adams Media, a division of F+W Media, Inc.
57 Littlefield Street, Avon, MA 02322. U.S.A.
www.adamsmedia.com

ISBN 10: 1-60550-626-5
ISBN 13: 978-1-60550-626-5
eISBN 10: 1-4405-0717-1
eISBN 13: 978-1-4405-0717-5

Printed in the United States of America.

10 9 8 7 6 5 4 3 2 1

Library of Congress Cataloging-in-Publication Data
is available from the publisher.

This publication is designed to provide accurate and authoritative information with
regard to the subject matter covered. It is sold with the understanding that the publisher is not engaged in rendering legal, accounting, or other professional advice.
If legal advice or other expert assistance is required, the services of a competent
professional person should be sought.
— From a *Declaration of Principles* jointly adopted by a Committee of the
American Bar Association and a Committee of Publishers and Associations

Many of the designations used by manufacturers and sellers to distinguish their
product are claimed as trademarks. Where those designations appear in this book
and Adams Media was aware of a trademark claim, the designations have been
printed with initial capital letters.

This book is available at quantity discounts for bulk purchases.
For information, please call 1-800-289-0963.

Dedicated to two saints:
My father, the late Neil Sokolowski,
the greatest man I'll ever know;
and Jude, the patron of the impossible.

"It doesn't get better, it doesn't get

worse, but it sure gets different!"

—David Lee Roth

CONTENTS

INTRODUCTION
The Accidental Adult 1

CHAPTER 1. Guyhood
An Off-ramp on the Road to Adulthood 9

CHAPTER 2. Work
The Ultimate Role-playing Game 23

CHAPTER 3. Music
This Is What You Call a *Mixtape* 47

CHAPTER 4. Suburbia
Keeping Your Poise 'n the Hood 59

CHAPTER 5. Entertaining
WTF? (Why Three Forks?) 73

CHAPTER 6. Parenting
Do as I Say, *Definitely* Not as I Do 99

CHAPTER 7. Transportation
SUVs and Minivans—It's How We Roll 113

CHAPTER 8. **Home Improvements**
Feeling Like a Tool 127

CHAPTER 9. **Civic Duties**
Caring So Little about So Much 141

CHAPTER 10. **Athletics**
Putting the Beer in Beer League 159

CHAPTER 11. **Hobbies**
"Adult" Entertainment (Not *That* Kind!). 177

CHAPTER 12. **Nostalgia**
Checking In with Your Inner Child. 203

CONCLUSION
Let's Stick Together. 217

ACKNOWLEDGMENTS

Adultlike gratitude goes to a triumvirate without whom this book might likely remain forever imprisoned on my laptop: Kurt Anderson, Katrina Schroeder, and über editor (and accidental adult apprentice) Brendan O'Neill. Your generosity and support will forever be appreciated. A cadre of super-talented authors held my hand along the way: Marya Hornbacher, Dan Zevin, Marc Parent, Kevin Revolinski, Alden Carter, and Dan Verdick. For their creative support and professional advice, appreciation goes to Katie Kelly Landberg, Jessica Hall Burns, Greg Helgeson, Carol Guensburg, Gordon Sumner, Ross Bernstein, Margo LaPanta, Pete Fabian, Sasha Aslanian, Lisa Gannaway, David Stillman, Mykl Roventine, my friends at The Loft Literary Center, my Spanish Harlem Mona Lisa, Wonder Dave, and Kieran's Irish Pub. Thanks go to my earliest team of reviewers: Mary and Eric Snustad, Kim and Mark Sacay, Donna and David Vanneste, Yachiyo and Rick Erickson, Lynda and Tom Savard, Molly Cave, and Emily Hawkins. For believing I could do this someday, I especially thank Brian Louis, Keri Kalfahs Pollock, Chuck and Sandi Shanle, Stacie Cronberg Lewis, Carlee Drummer, and Paula Kringle. Full-frontal hugs to my brothers James Cave, Steve Crosby, Patrick Dempsey, Chuck Hawkins, Matt Potter, Chris Stohl, Brian Strub, Tim Teuber, and the late, great Jeff Rhody. Special family love and thanks to mom Carolyn Jo, sister Megan, and brother Ryan for helping your baby boy kind of grow up and for always believing in me and humoring me; to Shanley, Finnegan, and Maeve for assuming I know what I'm doing and for teaching me that tranquility is overrated; and to Kelly for letting me turn around your Claddagh ring back in college and for joining me on this journey ever since. All my love.

THE
ACCIDENTAL
ADULT

f us never planned o
his happening. But it did
ometime between gra
chool and our first mort
age, a strange phenom
non began replacing ou
outhful mojos with
ew-found maturity. An
e didn't see it coming
ur two-door coupe
orphed into sliding
oor minivans. Bar-hop
ing turned into movi
ights on the couch. Nov
e write letters to th
ditor. And golfs. It's n

INTRODUCTION
The Accidental Adult

SOME OF US NEVER planned on this happening. But it did. Sometime between grad school and our first mortgage, strangely, our youthful mojo was replaced with a newfound maturity. And we didn't see it coming.

"It's not that I am afraid of getting old. I just want to get old in a certain way."

—Sting

Our two-door coupes morphed into sliding-door minivans. Bar hopping turned into movie nights on the couch. Late-night hookups with babes became early morning feedings with babies. And golf? It's not funny to suck anymore. For me, the transformation played out a little bit like this:

Aging college buddy, slurring into the phone: "It's a kegger, Colin! You have to drive up."

Lame excuse: "You know I'd love to, but gas prices are getting steep. And where am I going to sleep?"

Getting panicky over a party? When did I start caring if I'd crash on a couch or pass out on the floor? Such trivial concerns never used to bother me. Hell, I was the guy who'd never miss a party or diss his friends. Now I was doing both of those things. (And still using the word "diss.") Who am I becoming? I wondered. Where's that *carpe diem* spirit?

I'll tell you who I've become. Despite my best intentions to remain forever juvenile, I've instead grown reluctantly responsible and marginally mature. My life's biggest shocker? I've become an accidental adult. And I know I'm not alone.

DEFINING OUR TERMS

accidental adult (n.): An individual whose age indicates maturity but whose approach to life suggests otherwise.

What exactly makes someone an accidental adult? It's largely a matter of resistance. For most well-adjusted people, growing up isn't an unwelcome surprise. Many accept the inevitability of adulthood and embrace it. They resign themselves to lives of responsibility, serious endeavors, and a sensible wardrobe. They check their smoke alarm batteries twice a year. They know what kind of gas mileage their cars get. Some can even name their city councilperson.

But some of us join the world of adults kicking and screaming. Yes, technically we are adults. But more importantly, we are reluctant grownups who refuse to accept we're just like every other chump with credit card debt and an aching lower back. When we look in the mirror, the person we see staring back is decades younger and *way* cooler. We may spend an hour researching the best place to meet for a happy hour—you know, someplace not too noisy, with adequate restroom facilities, convenient parking, and a menu that accommodates our newly acquired shellfish allergy or gluten intolerance. But the point is, we still go, while many other adults hurry home to finish that drop ceiling in the new rec room. Are they conscientious? Absolutely. Fun? You tell me.

Life as an accidental adult may not be what we planned, but it's far more exciting than the existence of an everyday, garden-variety intentional adult. And it has many advantages. Friends don't call me to help them hang Sheetrock. I'm the one they call to answer late-night music trivia questions. No heavy lifting there. If a colleague needs a ride to work, I probably can't offer him a lift. My excuse? In good weather, I often commute on my 1986 motor scooter. And when the backyard parties start, no one expects me to build the best bonfire in the cul-de-sac. Guys like me hand a few sticks to the alpha males and then stand back at a safe distance chatting with the cute young wives while their inattentive husbands debate the ideal tinder assembly. Have at it guys. Some more wine, ladies?

So what is the opposite of an accidental adult?

assimilated adult (n.): One who embraces the responsibilities of adulthood without fearing the inevitable loss of a joyous, youthful soul.

You know these people. They're everywhere you look . . . in your neighborhood, at parties, at your kids' games, in line at the grocery store, and most certainly in your workplace. These are the adults who understand what society expects of them and do the right things the right way. They know how to get a better interest rate on their credit cards. They understand the proper ratio of comprehensive versus collision coverage on their auto insurance. They know what they pay in property taxes (every year). And to fill in those few holes where they lack the necessary knowledge, they've retained a group of adult subcontractors—their investor, their plumber, their lawyer, their personal trainer, their children's tutor, their caterer—to properly advise them along the way. Yes, their approach to life is always measure twice, cut once, while the accidental adult is more like, "Eh, that's about right."

ACTING MY AGE WITHOUT LOSING MY COOL

Some could say this approach to life seems irresponsible. So to avoid this criticism, it's sometimes necessary for us accidental adults to fit into the real-world adult cult as best we can. I call it "Acting my age without losing my cool." How does it work?

In the chapters that follow, I will offer you a handful of helpful tactics to employ when you absolutely, positively have to assimilate in order to earn credibility, respect, and legitimacy from your peers (even if they are lame-ass, adult sellouts).

What kind of survival strategies work best? That's for you to decide. But here's a preview of my favorite and perhaps the most versatile technique I can offer: *Embrace your inner smart-ass and fuel your inner monologue.* In action, it looks like this: Whenever necessary, try to project an outwardly adult appearance. In other words, act like you care while feigning interest in adultlike topics or issues whenever the need arises. At the same time, tap your inner insincerity, reminding yourself you're really not one of them and that's just fine.

Does this sound familiar?

Coworker on a warm day: "You know, it's not the heat. It's the humidity."

Outward response: "I suppose you're right about that!"

Inner monologue: *What a moron.*

Outraged neighbor: "Did you see what those punks built in my yard?"

Outward response: "Yeah, that's just sick. Who thinks a four-foot snow penis is funny?"

Inner monologue: *Nicely done guys! Great attention to detail.*

Parent at a children's dance recital: "I'm really impressed with the girls' hip-hop teacher."

Outward response: "Yes, she's very impressive."

Inner monologue: *Impressive indeed.*

Now who couldn't draw strength from a sanity system like this? See, I'm convinced everyone has a little inner monologue. It's just that us accidental adults have developed that voice into more of a primal scream than a whisper in order to survive these awkward, yet inevitable, assimilated adult interactions.

YOUR WORLD FRIGHTENS AND CONFUSES ME

Clearly, I'm not afraid to admit that I don't feel entirely comfortable in a world where it seems by now most adults understand things like umbrella insurance policies and Roth IRAs. In fact, that *Saturday*

Night Live skit where Unfrozen Caveman Lawyer confesses, "Your world frightens and confuses me," sums it up perfectly for me. Many days I feel like a thawed Neanderthal. It's like I've been awakened to a new era where people my age are now supposed to be accomplished, serious, and wise. Instead, I'm treading water in a sea of rising expectations and diminishing praise for accomplishments that are no longer considered spectacular but are now expected of me. And try as I might to fit in, the accidental adult in me still shines through. Consider these examples:

> *Instead of showing disgust at petty vandalism, I laugh whenever I see that someone has scratched an additional "Step 3: Wipe hands on pants" on the automatic hand dryer instructions in public restrooms.*

> *I don't usually wear an earring anymore, but I like to keep my options open. So about once a month, I force a metal stud through the closed-over puncture in my left earlobe. Sure, it bleeds, it stings, and it swells a little bit. But growing up is supposed to be painful, right?*

> *For me, the adult activity of lawn care is merely a painful obligation, a neighborhood courtesy, if you will. And unfortunately, I live on a street where the real men care a hell of a lot more than I do about the appearance of their lawns. How can you tell? Most of my neighbors wisely retained professional lawn-care services to properly fertilize their yards. But like any accidental adult, I fought this assimilation for years. Instead, I'd go out there and kick and curse that fertilizer cart as I dragged it haphazardly across my lawn. I only relented and hired a lawn-care pro after I accidentally burned a dozen jagged yellow stripes into my front*

lawn when the fertilizer spreader broke halfway through the job. For the better part of two months, I felt like the teenage son who ruined his daddy's lawn. But, hey, at least the burn pattern didn't spell out an obscene word. (Note to other accidental adults: repeatedly kicking a jammed fertilizer spreader does NOT ensure even application of the product.)

While the details might not match exactly, chances are you've had your own experiences that scream "accidental adult in action." Don't be embarrassed. The real adult world is a frightening and confusing place for people like us. But don't worry, you're running with the right crowd.

GOOD COMPANY

I'm willing to bet that a psychiatrist would tell me my perspective on adulthood is really just a coping mechanism to avoid the crushing reality that I'm a married man responsible for a mortgage, three young kids, and replacing the furnace filter regularly. Could be. And I suppose I'll get a therapist someday soon like other assimilated adults and find out for certain.

But in the meantime, I'm comfortable knowing that I'm in good company. And I even feel oddly mature realizing that some of my advice can help other reluctant grownups as well. I'm happy to help! Because every day I see evidence of other accidental adults like me—people my age who are capable, working professionals who don't feel confident handling jumper cables and who can't taste the difference between a Cabernet or a Chianti. People like you.

And the best part is, we really don't care. Why? Because we know life is too short to worry about succumbing to adult convention at every opportunity. If acting our age is going to mean losing our cool, I'm here to tell you it really doesn't have to be that way—especially when ignoring a few cultural standards and embracing our inner smart-ass can be tons more fun.

So sit back, hide this cover (pretend you're reading *The New Yorker* like a real grownup might), and prepare to learn a few techniques to help you muddle through your reluctant journey.

As we get older, we may not drive up for last-minute keggers as often as we used to—unless we can sneak in a little power nap first. But every day, accidental adults like us are navigating an important and sometimes perilous passage nonetheless: a crossing from the carefree playgrounds of the sophomoric life to the more solemn soils of adulthood. This may not be the roadtrip we had bargained for, but why not have a little fun along the way?

Now let's go, and enjoy the ride!

1. GUYHOOD

An Off-ramp on the Road to Adulthood

BEFORE WE START OFF, I should set a few things straight about my life and exactly how I turned into an accidental adult.

As the son of two college instructors, and the youngest of three siblings, I was coddled most of my life. And I fully appreciate this. Having other people do things for you is incredibly liberating. On family fishing trips, I never had to pilot the boat, nor did I care to. I got to sit back and lazily watch my bobber dip up and down while my dad maneuvered us into and out of the narrowest of fishing holes. During the heat of the summer, I spent more time in the cool of our basement playing my drum set than breaking a sweat doing yard work. Mom was right. It's just too dangerous for a thirteen-year-old to run the lawn mower. Isn't that what dads are for anyway?

During the Cub Scout years, I got a front-row seat to my dad's masterful production of several award-winning Pinewood Derby cars. After telling him my vision ("Make it look like a black cat, Dad!" or "This

"What kind of lives are these? We're like children. We're not men."

—Jerry Seinfeld

"No, we're not. We're not men."

—George Costanza, *Seinfeld*

[9]

year, I want a red racer!"), I was content to let da Vinci take over. He and I both knew I was really there just to hand him the wood glue or alert him whenever a precariously long ash threatened to break off the cigarette dangling from his lips and fall onto the soldering iron.

The flip side of all of this pampering is that I am now deep into my own twisted version of adulthood, and there are many typical "adult" things that are beyond my capacity, and certainly beyond my interest. A very partial list would include:

1. Driving a stick shift.
2. Grilling ribs.
3. Consistently applying a proper golf club grip.
4. Filleting a fish.
5. Placing a sports bet. (Should I play the over/under or just try to cover the spread?)
6. Properly preparing a mixed drink for a guest.
7. Smoking a cigar (without coughing).
8. Playing a hand of poker without asking questions.
9. Backing up a trailer.
10. Firing a shotgun.

Now, if you're an accidental adult like me and you share any of these incapacities, you probably don't care too much, otherwise you'd set about attempting to add these skills to your toolbox. What's preventing you? Some would say that demonstrating these proficiencies would bring themselves precariously closer to competing in the adult-cult contest where the guy who knows the most thinks he's the winner. Others would claim they feel comfortable enough in their own skin no matter how inept they may be. (Don't believe them most of the time.) For me, the reason I care so little about so much is simple: I've accepted the role of an accidental adult.

WELCOME TO GUYHOOD

In case you couldn't tell by now, I'm a lot more "guy" and a lot less "man," especially when it comes to what society considers typical adult male behavior, talents, and interests. Fortunately, being a guy (not a man) hasn't prevented me from leading a fairly normal life. I married a woman who is so stunning that she elevates my status with friends, coworkers, and random strangers walking down the street. When people meet my wife Kelly for the first time, I can practically read their minds as they think, "How did he pull that one off?" She's also funny, intelligent, and typically tolerant of my occasionally sophomoric sensibilities, which is nice. I'm also blessed to have three intelligent, kind, and acutely verbal kids. But despite this nuclear normalcy, my "I'm-a-guy-not-a-man" identity can make me feel a bit out of place in some situations. An unconventional guy like me can feel lost at times in a real man's world.

That's why I'm so lucky to have a solid group of college friends who have voluntarily joined me in taking up residence in our town of Guyhood (population: ten) while choosing to bypass Adulthood (population: most everyone else, it seems) instead.

Before I introduce you to this charming little hamlet, indulge me as I provide a brief history (and psychology) lesson.

THE ID KIDS

If you weren't hung over during Psych 101, you might recall Sigmund Freud's concept of the *id*. He described this part of our psyche as the division ruled by the pleasure-pain principle. If it feels good, you go for it. If it hurts, you don't bother. (This illustrates the scientific reasoning behind my napping instead of weed-whacking most any Saturday afternoon.) The id is completely illogical, primarily sexual, infantile in its emotional development, and it will not take no for an answer. It does not take social norms into account when thinking or acting.

In defining the id, I think Freud was also describing my circle of college friends, or as I like to call them, the Id Kids. And if you're an accidental adult like me, chances are you have friends who are a lot like mine.

BRIAN: THE CRAP COLLECTOR

First meet Brian. When I did, he was the king of kids—a true accidental adult in training. A quick survey of his dorm room told it all. Stuffed animals, action-figures, posters, and T-shirts adorned his room featuring everyone from Homer Simpson to Cap'n Crunch to ALF to Spuds MacKenzie to Max Headroom. There wasn't a cheesy, dated, pop-culture icon or figurine he didn't have, with the exception of maybe a *Land of the Lost* Sleestak (and I'm sure that's not for lack of trying). In a time when guys tried to score by drowning themselves in Drakkar Noir and plying girls with Bartles & Jaymes wine coolers, Brian thought shitty trinkets and cartoon crap were his tickets to paradise. Fast forward to today, and he's a married father of two whose home now features a room devoted to displaying much of the same junk he collected back in college. I should know. I've helped him move crates of that crap more than a few times.

JAMES: THE NONCONFORMIST

Now I give you James, formerly known as Jim. In college, Jim was the roommate you'd walk in on as he was standing at the mirror with an eyeliner pen in his hand. Sure, he attributed his grooming proclivities to influences such as The Cure and *Pretty in Pink* and *Edward Scissorhands*, but his behavior really just boiled down to his wanting to be different. Jim was the one who'd stop talking for half a day just to try a vow of silence, or the one who'd bring his date wilted daisies because he thought that was a peculiarly charming gesture. Decades later, his affinity for the antiadult world shines through stronger than ever, and he's still fighting convention. He has shaved his head, pierced his ears, sports dozens of tattoos, and now bears a striking resemblance to Jesse "the Body" Ventura, although James would tell you he owned that look first. At the baptism of his first son, the officiating priest instructed James and his wife Molly to simply reply, "Yes," when asked the standard litany of questions like, "Do you reject Satan?" and "Will you raise your child in a God-centered home?" In other words, they asked him to conform to convention. Nope, not James. Instead of placating the priest, James pulled a crumpled piece of paper from his baggy David Byrne/Talking Heads sport coat pocket and read his prepared statement, announcing, "We are committed to raising our son in a world of diversity with respect, peace, and love for all of God's creations." Blah, blah, blah. Hey, that's great, James! But this is the Catholic Church. Play along, please. Unfortunately, that's what adults are supposed to do sometimes.

RHODES: THE BRILLIANT BUT CONFUSED

Finally, let me introduce you to Rhodes, although I'm fairly sure you already know him. He's often the most intelligent person in the room, but you couldn't tell by his demeanor. All his life he was the poster child for Freud's concept of the id, especially the "disregard for social norms" part: lived with his parents well into his thirties . . . wandered in and out of jobs . . . never picked up a bar tab . . . often disheveled, disoriented, and confused, even when sober . . . always needed a ride somewhere . . . never brought his ID to the bars . . . couldn't provide a straight answer to the most routine of questions . . . best friend is his dog.

To me he's the lovable, loyal, intelligent yet oblivious Rhodes, but *your* "Rhodes" is probably named Schmidty, or Sully, or Coop. He may be the last person you'd invite to a wine and cheese soiree, but after a few of those painful adult party conversations with assimilated adults, you'd wish you were eating sloppy joes and drinking Special Ex with him instead.

LAUGHTER EVER AFTER

Do my friends sound familiar? That's probably because we accidental adults share the same fundamental perspective: There's safety in numbers. And in a world filled with professional adults, we amateurs need to stick together. Fortunately for many of us, we find these kindred spirits early in our lives and hang onto them for dear life.

When my friends and I graduated from college, many of us Id Kids moved into single-room apartments in different cities around the country. There was little to prepare us for the transition from the nonstop chaotic party atmosphere of college life to the solitary confinement of a studio apartment in a town where we knew hardly anyone. After too many solitary meals in front of the TV, we began to imagine ourselves choking on a chicken bone and having to self administer the Heimlich maneuver by throwing our diaphragms onto the corners of our tables. For those of us who couldn't afford furniture, death was the imagined and darkly hilarious outcome. This, of course, all led to arguments over which one of us could go the longest dead and undiscovered in his apartment.

Even though the college years are a few decades behind us now, and we live much closer to each other, our humor has never graduated. In fact, it's a primary reason we all enjoy each other's company as much as we do. Most people are probably guilty of forwarding the occasional off-color e-mail or hyperlink to friends and family, but for accidental adults like me and my friends . . . well . . . infantile, lowbrow, crotch-grabbing humor isn't the exception. It's usually our rule.

So what's still funny to us in Guyhood? If your grown-up life has you feeling more mature than you'd like, try any one of these activities, and you'll find yourself back down on more comfortable, familiar ground in no time.

COZY CRUISING

To play, you get two guys to agree to share the front seat of a car with you for a spin around town. Very important note: You want to be the passenger next to the window. Why? When the car approaches a woman, you tell the driver to honk the horn to get her attention. When she looks up to see who's admiring her, you duck down to the floor, leaving your buddies as the only two visible occupants of the car—a waving driver and his middle-seat passenger who appear to be on a very cozy date.

PHONY PHONE MESSAGES

Long before Bart Simpson started prank calling Moe's Tavern, my group of friends used similar tactics to embarrass each other, especially during the first years of our entry-level careers. We found that nothing says "professionalism" quite like the experience of rushing through a hectic day at work only to have a colleague interrupt your meeting to say you have an urgent call from Dick Fitzenwell.

Or that Phil McCracken says he's running late for your lunch with Jack Hoffer. Amazingly, these never get old.

SHE'S *SO* LOOKING AT YOU, DUDE

Years ago, we thought nothing of flirting with the server at our favorite bar or asking her, "Which one of us do you think is the most attractive?" Fortunately, marriage has matured most of us to the point where we now participate in safer games—like convincing a friend that a woman is checking him out when evidence (or lack thereof) would suggest otherwise. Here's how to do it. When he returns from the bathroom, tell your target that the brunette by the pool tables tracked him the whole way. Or when the cute server leaves after taking the table's order, simply offer up a, "Well, I know who's getting his food first! Did you see how she brushed up against you when she collected the menus?" You'll find it takes surprisingly little effort to confound his logic, falsely boost his ego, and entertain your friends, especially if the victim so desperately wants to believe he's still legit.

BACKHANDED COMPLIMENTS

Nothing smacks of insincerity quite like the halfhearted praise my friends and I often lavish upon each other. Want to send your friend a backhanded compliment? Whenever a party guest is acting particularly lame, tell him, "I really have a blast around you! You make me feel like the life of the party!" When a coworker bungles an important project, tell her, "Thank you for leading our team! You really make me feel smart!" Anytime you and your friends are dressed up for a formal event, be sure to admit, "It's always

great going out with you. I feel attractive whenever I'm with you!"
And whenever a buddy is violently attacking an extreme platter of
nachos or onion rings, it's quite okay to tell him, "You make me feel
healthy!" However, be prepared that remarks like these are usually
acknowledged with a smile and a single-finger salute.

HIT AND RUNS

The goal here is to interject quick, uncomfortable comments in
front of as large an audience as possible:

- At sporting events: "Look-it, that coach's nuts!"
- When entering public bathrooms already occupied by friends,
  and more importantly, strangers: "Who wants to earn $5?"
- When talking about your jobs: "How many people work on
  your staff?"
- When walking past crowded construction sites: "When did
  that steel erection pop up?"
- When announcing Saturday afternoon errands: "Good news,
  guys! My wife is sending me to the fabric store. I'm gonna
  get felt!"

Yes, we're guilty of spectacular immaturity in Guyhood. But this
juvenile behavior would seem much worse if we behaved this way
all the time instead of safely reverting to ignorance of social norms
whenever we convene. We often imagine what real adults talk about
over gin and tonics. Probably the stock market, or their golf handi-
cap, or the role deregulation played in the foreclosure crisis. Why do
I think this? Because I've had the displeasure of sitting in on a few
of those conversations, trying to play along. But for us Id Kids, it's a

pitcher of the beer on special and a race to see who can find photos of the attractive local newscaster on their cell phones. Or a competition over who's tasted the most obscure microbrew. Or a debate over which Disney princess we'd most like to nail, and why.

COMPENSATE THROUGH SENSITIVITY

To be fair, I should explain that nowadays Guyhood is more of a vacation destination. Like most spots, it offers us a fleeting but necessary chance to rest, unwind, and cope. It's certainly not our permanent home, and I wouldn't suggest you consider a permanent relocation, either. But I would like to sell you on a few amenities we've established that make me proud to be "one of the guys." Because as immature as we may seem, Guyhood offers us a level of benefits much deeper than junior high jokes that makes it worth visiting from time to time.

HUG IT OUT

Forget those manly death-grip "Good to see you" handshakes, keeping acquaintances at arm's length. Full-frontal hugs are the rule for us . . . in parking lots, movie theater lobbies, restaurants, golf clubhouses . . . wherever.

**ACCIDENTAL ADULT
ADVICE ALERT**

Hugging a good friend in public won't kill you. In some cultures, men hold hands or walk arm in arm. Now how about that?

PRESENCE, NOT PRESENTS

When our children have birthday parties or baptisms or First Communions, we don't just send a card. We go to our friends' houses, eat their ham salad sandwiches, and play with the kids in the sandbox.

ACCIDENTAL ADULT
ADVICE ALERT

Spending quality time with a friend's family endears you to the spouse. Remember her? She's the gatekeeper who determines if your buddy can meet you at Rib Fest again this summer.

CHEAP THERAPY

A lot of men are reluctant to share personal problems with friends for fear of looking weak. This is not so when you're in the Guyhood nest. Whether it's a rough time at work or a spat with a spouse, it's reassuring to know you have friends who really care and are ready to offer any advice or help necessary. Sure you're prone to siding with your buddies more often than not, but you're also close enough friends to call a dick "a dick" when tough love is in order as well.

ACCIDENTAL ADULT
ADVICE ALERT

Let's be honest. Your life is going to suck from time to time, especially when you're partially responsible for a share of someone else's happiness and you're busy staring down a quarter-life or midlife crisis of your own. When the chips are down and a friend needs a little support, pick up the phone or send a supportive e-mail (maybe with a link to an inappropriate YouTube video at the end). This kind of bold move shows some much-needed sensitivity, considering you're the one who regularly invites your friend to have sex with himself whenever he pisses you off.

SAVE THE DATE

In our circle, the first Wednesday of the month is known as Guys' Movie Night. By now, it's become a somewhat sacred tradition where each guy takes a turn choosing the happy-hour spot, the movie to see, and the bar to visit after the movie. Those who can't attend are duly chastised for disrespecting the custom. (Those who pick lame movies are also castigated, but less so . . . .)

ACCIDENTAL ADULT
ADVICE ALERT

You know that calendar in your kitchen where your wife posts silly notes like "Be home on time—it's your turn to drive the girls to dance class" or "Call TiVo today to cancel service"? Well, try using that funny little grid to schedule a regular tradition with friends. Without an established event, getting together can often slide to the back burner.

SAY IT!

When someone's having a rough time or struggling with something significant, we're not afraid to say, "I'm praying for you," or even, "I love you," without feeling the need to add the word "man" at the end.

ACCIDENTAL ADULT
ADVICE ALERT

No one is immune from the occasional bump in the road. When you see a pal in need, don't underestimate your ability to make a difference. I know you forgot that id lesson from college, but you don't need a degree in psychotherapy to lift up a friend.

THAT GUY'S NUTS

No, we're not "men" by the conventional meaning of the word. But like the characters on *Seinfeld*, my friends and I find comfort in knowing that at least we're in good company. When we're together there's no pretending. No one's embarrassed to admit he doesn't quite understand the terms of his credit card. And he's even guy enough to ask for help figuring them out. If our roadtrip car died on the side of the highway, we wouldn't bother to prop up the hood and pretend to look around. We'd call AAA on speed dial (if we were responsible men who actually had AAA) and head to the nearest townie bar to await adult rescue.

But maybe what's most important for any accidental adult is simply to know the time and place for checking into and out of Guyhood. (You probably won't land spouses or significant others if you don't.) And it will be a tribute to your genuine friendships when you and your friends can really truly be yourselves around each other. I often think how sad it must be for the guy who wants to laugh at an immature joke, or who'd rather order a pint of beer than a glass of Merlot but doesn't for fear of looking unadult to his buddy. I'm sure he has a better feel for classic adulthood than us accidental adults. But you know what we say to that? "That man's nuts! Grab 'm!"

f us never planned o
is happening. But it di
ometime between gra
chool and our first mort
age, a strange phenom
non began replacing ou
outhful mojos with
ew-found maturity. An
e didn't see it coming
ur two-door coupe
orphed into sliding
oor minivans. Bar-hop
ing turned into movi
ights on the couch. No
e write letters to th
iter. And golfs. It's n

2. WORK

The Ultimate Role-playing Game

THERE'S A MOMENT IN every accidental adult's life when you catch yourself saying something really strange, something adultlike that you never thought you'd hear yourself utter. And when you do, it feels like an out-of-body experience reflecting a maturity you never anticipated. Phrases like "Great news, honey! The Feds lowered interest rates today!" or "Damn kids! Get off my lawn!"

For me, those unanticipated words were "Please pass your papers to the front of the class."

"What if we're still doin' this when we're fifty?"

—Peter Gibbons, *Office Space*

SECRETS OF YOUR SUCCESS?

Discovering that I had become a teacher (albeit temporarily) was quite the shocker for me as a young adult. But since then, I've realized that simply joining the working world itself—regardless of the occupation—is fraught with peril, especially for accidental adults. Back in the day, strangers at parties would ask you, "So what's your major?" just to harmlessly evaluate your fun factor. Now the question has become a much more serious, "So what do you do?"—as if the answer will cleanly define all the complexities of who you currently are. And like it or not, your answer to that question typically leads directly to a silent judgment that deems you nerdy or boring or cool or rich or smart or lazy or risky or incompetent.

Like most of my friends, I've worked a handful of jobs since graduating from the comfortable confines of college. I might not have held enough positions to qualify me as a career coach, but the jobs I've had have broken my spirit sufficiently enough that I can now help you, my fellow accidental adult—if you'll let me.

– – –

If you're looking for an inspiring fish-tales metaphor to help transform you into a positive, productive employee, like those salmon-tossing fishmongers at Pike Place Market in Seattle . . . well, this isn't that book. If you're hoping to learn how to win friends and influence people, there's a better business classic out there (I wish I could remember its name). And if you're craving more nuggets of witty advice like your commencement speaker's recommendation to "wear sunscreen," this isn't it. But if all you need is a few practical coping mechanisms beyond banal advice like "Play boardroom bingo!" or "Avoid stress!" then read on. It's been years since I've stood in front of a classroom, but I'll bet I've got a lesson or two that, when properly applied, could very well blossom into the secrets of your success someday.

So . . . would you kindly take your seats, and if someone would please get the door? Class is now in session . . . and the first lesson comes from history.

THE SPEECH TEACH

The first detour on my reluctant journey to adulthood was a two-year pit stop commonly referred to as grad school. While I wanted to boost my career income potential, I also wasn't exactly ready for the daily grind of the adult-cult rat race. So after a miserable year of postundergrad employment, I moved back in with my parents, and I traded my entry-level job for a graduate teaching assistantship. Yes, I joined the noble ranks of academia's most esteemed crowd: the TAs.

First, let me dispel some of the common myths about teaching assistants. They don't merely assist tenured professors with grading exams or photocopying syllabi. And they don't all sleep with their professors. Or their students. At least not in my case. My teaching assistantship meant preparing and delivering original twice-a-week lectures for three classes of twenty-eight students who were taking a required course called Introduction to Oral Communication 101. Some simply called it Speech. Many called it That-Dumb-Ass-Three-Credit-Course-I-Need-in-Order-to-Graduate. Of course, my super-mature college buddies just called it Oral. "Hey Colin, I heard you're teaching Oral. Good for you! How's that going?"

Yes funny stuff. Unless it's *you* who's struggling to establish credibility and respect as a young professional—while also hoping your students think you're cooler than the real adult professors who deliver the weekly large-group seminar. Unless it's *you* who has to wear a tie every day just so any passerby glancing through the classroom doorway can distinguish the teacher from the students. Unless it's *you* who has to sit straight-faced and feign maturity while listening to countless speeches on riveting topics like "How to create a fake ID," or "Why senior citizens shouldn't drive," or "Three steps to beating any breathalyzer."

Not only did I have to evaluate hundreds of these speeches each semester, but I also was required to read midterm papers, deliver and grade final exams, and, best of all, use discretion! All at the ripe old age of twenty-three.

If you're thinking there's something very wrong with all of this, I couldn't agree more. I mean, what's less cool than a broke-ass guy who's living at home and teaching students who are almost as old as he is? Not much. And what's more dangerous than any twenty-three-year-old applying academic discretion to twenty-one-year-olds? Again, not much. And what's more unfair than asking a guy to ignore the fact that many of his coed students are really cute, unless he wants a lawsuit and a prompt dismissal from the university? I think you know the answer.

If you'd say all of that is a lot to ask of an accidental adult, what do you think the students thought?

FROM THE MOUTHS OF BABES

"Are you, like, the teacher?"

My first day of class, I fielded that seemingly simple question repeatedly. But believe it or not, the answer was a bit complicated. Thankfully, my public relations skills were blossoming, and I had a handy nonanswer reply at the ready.

"Well, you'll go to the lecture hall once a week for the main lecture, and you'll come here twice a week to give your speeches. Then I'll reinforce the lecture and lead our small group in some discussions."

"No, I mean, like, who gives us our grades?"

Ah. Cutting to the chase.

"Um, that would be me." I wanted to add, "Using my discretion!" But I left it at that. They had no idea how eager I was to wield discretion. And of all the classes I could have taught, probably none offered more opportunities to evaluate students using arbitrary, capricious judgment calls than Speech 101. Each day, groups of four students would deliver seven-minute original speeches on any topic they chose. I'd sit in the back of the room and evaluate them on organization, delivery, visual aids, references, and overall performance. Were they loud enough? Well organized? Did they signal their conclusion? Use transitions? Stare at their notes? Discretion, discretion, discretion! It was amazing what I could do! From their lips to my immature mind to a grade I recorded to their academic records . . . forever! What a progression of power—and the opportunities to exercise discretion seemed endless.

There were informational speeches, demonstration speeches, persuasive speeches, and everyone's favorite, impromptu speeches. On "Impromptu Fridays," I'd fill a box with speech topics like "What career are you pursuing and why?" or "Your roommate just won an award. Deliver the introduction speech." Students had about two minutes to gather their thoughts before performing a ninety-second speech complete with an introduction (always a good idea), a structured body (think: rambling), and finally a conclusion (mercifully). For their entertaining efforts, all were rewarded with miniature Snickers bars given by their very generous TA whose mother (and landlord) bought the candies for her baby boy the night before. For the students, these off-the-cuff orations were both harrowing and hysterical. For me, the speeches were often difficult to distinguish from the other required speeches largely because many of the students once again delivered performances that were pulled out of their asses.

But I wasn't alone in exercising discretion. Each semester, my students completed teacher evaluation forms telling me and my faculty advisor what they thought of *my* performance. To my surprise, turns out most of my students saw a confident, easygoing, and helpful teacher. But the great secret of my little academic adventure was that inside I felt inadequate and ill-prepared for an adult's profession. To compensate, I took my job very seriously, probably too seriously. I offered my home phone number on the syllabus so I could always be available for students. (I prayed my mother wouldn't answer those calls, forcing me to explain that, yeah, I'm living at home with my parents, but I'm still your teacher.) I'd regularly stay after class working with students on their delivery techniques and brainstorming topics with them. Yet I was such a white-knuckled worrier that minutes before most classes I could be found in the bathroom fighting a recurring case of the nerves. *What if today's the day they find out I'm a fraud? What if they challenge my feedback? What if I projectile vomit?*

Fortunately for me, the only ones humiliated in my classroom were the students, never the teacher. And really, who's to blame for that? Kids who prepared adequately usually did fine. And the students who weren't ready to deliver a speech? Well, they faced the wrath of peer feedback sessions, diplomatically moderated by *moi*:

"I counted thirteen for Kristen today," Funny Freshman Ted would report. We called Ted the Wizard of Ahhs because he kept a tally of how many "ums" or "ahhs" everyone used.

"Thank you, Ted. Kristen, I think what Ted is telling us is that you could use some practice leaving silent gaps between your sentences, rather than filling the spaces with nervous interjections."

Or...

"He just stared at me," Sorority Snob Bridget would complain.

"Hey Jake, Bridget's right. Eye contact is very important in establishing a bond with your audience. Please work on varying your attention around the room."

Yet even while fighting my own butterflies and dispensing critiques of speeches with forced maturity, my inner smart-ass ramped up its own silent response to my students' performances.

Outward response: "A few stumbles here and there, but I'm proud of your effort."

Inner monologue: *I'm embarrassed for you.*

Or...

Outward response: "You have a really strong presence. And a wonderful speaking voice."

Inner monologue: *You are so sweet. Keep your eye contact locked this way please.*

Or...

Outward response: "Don't forget to identify your sources."

Inner monologue: *We both know you're making this shit up.*

Each semester things got better. My confidence grew when I saw that students respected me more and challenged me less. Their evaluations of my teaching were solid, with several comments indicating that *I* had made *them* feel comfortable. (Imagine that!) I even started to think I had a reasonable chance to win the Teacher of the Year award given to the top TA every spring. It was possible. I mean, consider my competition:

- A blonde bisexual hottie who proved quite popular with the male students. Funny how that works. But her habit of dating students didn't play well with the faculty advisor.
- An extremely polite but painfully inarticulate woman who could barely speak English, let alone objectively grade speeches given in her second language.
- A disdainful young conservative who seldom disguised his severely pious and judgmental viewpoints. Not too cool with the overwhelmingly liberal students on most college campuses.

With one semester to go until I had completed my assistantship, I was amazed and delighted to discover I was looking like a shoe-in for the top prize. Then I met Ed.

CAN YOU HEAR THE FEAR?

At first glance, you might think Ed was like all the other male undergrad students in central Wisconsin during the mid 1990s. Zebra-striped Zubaz? Check. Mullet? Check. Untied, oversized Chuck Taylors? Double check.

But there was something different about Ed that I immediately noticed the first day of the new semester. As students began to fill the room, Ed was already sitting in the front row. I wondered if he was eagerly awaiting my now standard opening lecture—the one where I explain that in poll after poll, public speaking ranks as one of people's top fears (usually in second place behind dying). And since I anticipated that no students would actually kick the bucket during my class, they should be proud that they were about to tackle the thing they probably feared the most. Brilliant oratory to be sure.

Anyway, as Ed faced forward from the front row of desks, a middle-aged woman was seated in a chair positioned directly in front of him, with her back to me, and she was energetically motioning her hands while Ed paid close attention. As the woman got up to approach me, my heart rate accelerated. I already knew what she was about to explain. "Here's a curveball, sucker! To hell with your Teacher of the Year award! Mess this up, and you'll ruin this poor kid for life!"

Yes, Ed had a hearing problem. Except he wasn't hard of hearing. Ed was deaf. But as his interpreter explained to me, I was to simply treat Ed like all the other students.

Right. Except he's in a speech class. And he can't hear the words he's speaking, so could I give him help honing his delivery skills? And he can't read my lips if I turn to face the whiteboard, so could I try to always face the class whenever I'm speaking? And it's difficult for him to take notes while he's reading teachers' lips, so could I find another student to share notes with him? And sometimes when he smiles, his facial muscles activate a sensor in his hearing aids and it emits a high-pitched squeal, so could I explain that to the class so they're not alarmed if the noise interrupts their speeches (because it really only means Ed's smiling so he must have liked something they said)?

Of course I can! I can also find my faculty advisor to find out what the hell he was thinking when he thought this young TA was capable of accommodating this student's needs. And when I did, immediately after the first class, he shrugged it off. "You'll do fine with him, and he'll do fine with you."

I don't know the exact sign language for "Thanks for nothing!" but I wished I could have shared it with Professor Glib.

Maybe the class knew I felt I was in over my head. Maybe Ed did, too. But they never let on. Instead, to my surprise, everyone seemed to rise to the occasion. When Ed delivered his first speech, I was more on edge than he was. I hoped he'd perform well, but I felt like I had a front-row ticket to a potential train wreck.

But to my relief and amazement, Ed did just fine. Like most nervous students, he spoke a bit too rapidly, but his words were clear. He smiled a lot. And most importantly, his personality came shining through, revealing himself to be a very likeable and funny kid. At the speech's conclusion, the class gave him a wildly enthusiastic reception, overplaying their applause for his visual benefit.

Throughout the semester, Ed continued to stand in front of his peers and deliver short, C-worthy speeches. Seeing no preferential treatment of Ed, his classmates gave him honest feedback, both positive and negative. And as time went on, I realized Ed didn't need any special treatment. I just needed to treat him like any other student in my classroom.

By the end of the semester, I forgot I was a kid teaching kids. No one exposed me as an adult imposter. No one caught on that an accidental adult was leading the class. My students respected me (at least to my face), my faculty advisor entrusted Ed with me, and yes, in the end (drum roll please . . .) I did receive the highly coveted (by me) TA Teacher of the Year award.

AWARD? WON. BATTLE? LOST.

The day I learned the award was mine turned out to be the exact same day I realized I had unwittingly succeeded in pulling off my first professional adult charade. That morning I was studying in the university library when a student of mine spotted me reading at a table. I looked up, and we exchanged a polite hello, then she moved along to her destination. No big deal, right? Wrong. When I saw her in my class later that afternoon, she lingered in the classroom afterwards just to tell me, "Remember when I saw you in the library this morning? That was funny!"

My polite smile evaporated into a halfhearted grin, barely disguising my growing disappointment.

Funny? Like when you're six years old and you see your first-grade teacher at McDonald's and your parents have to explain to you that teachers are real people who eat food too? Funny like when you see your principal wearing a T-shirt and shorts at the mall, and you can't believe the guy would ever be without a necktie?

No, "funny" is *not* seeing a guy roughly the age of your older brother sitting in a campus library. Have I really become one of *those* people to my students? A professional adult void of any youthfully relatable characteristics, operating on a completely foreign plane?

The evidence would suggest I indeed had morphed into an accidental adult. Somewhere between my cold-sweat episodes and my juvenile inner monologues from the back of the classroom, my advisor deemed me award-winning and my students considered me credible. Sure that's an honor to any well-adjusted young professional anxious to join the real world, but it's also something of a burden to a reluctant grownup struggling against the inevitable pull of the adult cult.

DID I JUST SAY THAT?

Clearly, coming to grips with a new vocation-formed identity remains hard to swallow for many accidental adults. So what's a young professional to do when you're suddenly considered a colleague of middle-aged coworkers? Are you really expected to swap "How was your weekend?" stories on Monday mornings when your account might make your officemates blush? Are you succumbing to adulthood or just sucking up by telling your boss you spent your vacation reading his gifted copy of *Who Moved My Cheese?* And is deep, lasting, self-loathing an appropriate reaction the first time you hear yourself mutter, "Thank God, it's Friday . . . all day!" as you refill your coffee cup at the water cooler?

If you're shocked and saddened to discover your bottom's on the line for your company's bottom line, or if you feel like your occupation itself is a hazard (to your truest identity), then take my advice. Don't resign. Instead, simply resign yourself to a lifetime of performing involuntary servitude with the best attitude possible and, when necessary, a little bit of professional posturing for sanity's sake. Sound like a tall order? Maybe this memo can help.

M E M O

TO: Early to midcareer accidental adults

FROM: Colin Sokolowski

RE: A new paradigm for workplace sanity

It has come to my attention that you have taken on a new responsibility for which you feel unprepared. This exhausting undertaking, often referred to as a "job," now demands that you associate with people much older than you for up to eight to ten hours a day while collaborating on projects that are at times miles away from your soul's deepest yearnings. I am also aware that this financially necessary circumstance occasionally

forces awkward social interactions with super-serious
coworkers who employ an odd new vocabulary that requires
you to know the definition of words like "synergy" and
"leverage"—whereas it is painfully obvious that it is
unimportant for them to know what it means when you say
"I need to get out of this circle jerk" or "this project
is officially FUBAR" to describe work's most infuriating
situations.

If you're like me, this situation presents a unique
challenge. You'd like to preserve your delusional self-
identity that says you're much cooler and more exciting
than your humdrum work environment allows you to
display. Yet you can't exactly force your unbridled life
philosophies down your colleagues' throats, unless you
want to be unceremoniously shit-canned from your job.
So how can you convey your personality at work without
compromising your soul?

Clearly, this commission calls for a shift in your
mindset in order to maintain a modicum of workplace
sanity. If successful, you will be able to perform at
levels high enough to ensure you earn a salary that
allows you to purchase life's necessities like concert
tickets, gas for weekend roadtrips, and enough beer to
keep the summer barbecues going into the night. If you're
unsuccessful because you've chosen to set free your
rampant sense of individuality at every opportunity, well
. . . you may feel like you have won the nonconformity
lottery, but your wallet and marriage will likely pay the
price.

Therefore, effective immediately, I require you to review the following paradigm I've developed to enhance your core competencies at work while keeping your sanity in check. The details of this model are outlined below.

BEST PRACTICES FOR OFFICE SUCCESS AND SANITY

DON'T DRIVEL

I've spent the better part of my working years trying to find the right words for every audience in every situation (although Kelly would challenge how wisely I choose my words at home). Anyway, I can confidently tell you that there's a fine line between exhibiting an excellent command of the English language and merely demonstrating that you're a mindless robot capable of spewing the most meaningless business jargon ever invented.

I think we've all worked with that guy whose favorite phrases are "Value-added!" "Results-driven!" and "Client-centric!" He never simply presents a new product or initiative. Where's the drama in that? Nope, it's a "Launch!" or a "Roll Out!" He never wants to revisit a topic for another day. He'd much rather "Circle back" with you instead. When he needs to show you how to navigate his "forward-thinking" website, he doesn't instruct you to simply click through a series of hyperlinks. Instead, you must "drill down" to find the data. And when his supervisors stop by, it's not a meeting with his bosses. It's a summoning by "The Brass!" or "Corporate!" Yes, we're glad this cube monkey who just loves to "Network!" has a firm grip on the obvious along with an arsenal of tired phrases at the ready. But believe me: The person who prattles on like the smartest person in the room usually isn't.

ALWAYS LOOK BUSY

Never walk down a hallway without a bulging, overstuffed folder under your arm. Carrying papers with you at all times tells your colleagues "I'm on my way to an important meeting with my thoughtful analysis and comprehensive response to resolve the crisis." But in your haste, be careful not to clip a coworker coming around the corner. Your scattered papers littering the hallway now reveal you were on a five-minute aimless walk around the office corridors with your trusty fantasy football folder of draft picks, players' statistics, and trade requests.

SEND LATE-NIGHT E-MAILS

You don't need an MBA (or the much more prestigious master of arts in communications) to pull off this trick. In fact, it's so old school, it's more like a lesson from Marketing 100, the prerequisite to Marketing 101. It's simple really. Sometime between your fifth Rolling Rock of the night and stumbling into bed, log into your work e-mail account and blast off a few carefully typed messages for your supervisor or anyone else whom you'd like to impress. Regardless of your actual activities at the moment (television), keeping your messages work related (not focused on your keen observation that you and your buddies are so like the guys on *Entourage*) is always a good idea.

EXPERIENCE UNEXPECTED PHONE TROUBLES

I wish I could take credit for this ingenious stunt, but it comes from a much more jaded and broken coworker than myself. Every now and then, you've likely experienced the misfortune of enduring an unpleasant phone call from a client or customer who is berating and blaming you for all of society's ills. The latest computer virus? You started it. The subprime mortgage crisis? Your loan triggered it. Had enough of this unwarranted tirade? Of course you have! But business etiquette suggests you can't exactly hang up on another person. Or could you? According to my cynical colleague, it all depends on *when* you terminate the call. His suggestion? Launch into what seems like a heartfelt apology and in midsentence hang up on yourself. The brilliance in this maneuver is that the caller will assume you've had phone troubles. Who would intentionally disconnect a phone call while they're talking?

BEWARE OF THE PROFESSIONAL PROFESSIONALS

You know that old saying reserved for life's most annoying people "There's one in every crowd"? Well at most of the professional conferences I go to, there's more like three or four—one for each of the seminars I attend. These are the people whose sole purpose in life is to attend professional organization events just so they can interrupt the speakers to interject obvious observations or nonrelevant questions that ultimately bring the presentations to a screeching halt, all at the bewilderment of the rest of us who actually wanted to hear the expert speak. I'm willing to bet that these professional professionals are actually mediocre workers back in their humble offices. Yet you bring them into a group setting and suddenly these pompous brown-nosers hold delusions of competency, convinced that their unrequested commentary is actually advancing the group's discussion when in reality the speaker and audience are sharing a collective and unspoken "shut the hell up" reaction.

Once you spot these haughty fools at the morning keynote address, put a few rows of distance between you and them for the rest of the day, and avoid eye contact at all costs. If you're feeling especially brazen, immediately follow up one of their asinine digressions by taking the microphone, shaking your head, and offering the speaker a "Sorry about that . . . ." Then launch into an inquiry of actual substance. Your fellow conferencegoers will revere you, and those fuming professional professionals will revile you. Nicely played!

TAKE A SEAT (AWAY)

During my first job out of college, I worked with a socially stunted middle-aged man who talked incessantly about the NFL draft no matter the time of year. He was so engrossed in sharing with me his concerns over Green Bay's potential seventh-round pick that he became oblivious to all of my nonverbal cues (crossed arms, flared nostrils, rapid breathing) telling him I didn't give a frog's fat ass what the Packers did during the offseason. Before I knew it, damn near every cubicle visit from this drone would eat up about an hour of my time—time that could have been better spent needlessly mentoring Cara, the cute college intern. Enraged at this injustice, I finally got creative.

My solution? A suddenly cluttered visitor chair at the end of my desk. It works like this. When you see or hear any undesirable coworker approaching your office, immediately stack up a pile of papers and folders on your guest chairs so your advancing colleague can't sit down. Sure, his inane stand-up monologue will still rob you of a few precious moments of your life. But eventually his arch supports will give out, and he'll leave in search of a more comfortable office from which to hold court, effectively cutting his unsolicited visit to your office at least in half. Conversely, don't forget to immediately clear off your chair when you hear Cara, the cute college intern, approaching. You wouldn't want to miss her office rounds at 9 A.M. on Mondays when she offers salacious recaps of her girlfriends' weekend escapades. But try not to look too obvious or overly anxious by rushing to your chair and sweeping it free of clutter with one broad stroke of your arm, knocking books and folders to the floor. Just be glad she might even consider talking to you. If you weren't her internship advisor, you know you'd be SOL.

USE DECORUM WHEN DECORATING

If it's true that your desk space reflects both your personality and your professionalism, then I'm in no position to offer you decorating advice. Let's take a look around my workstation: a set of miniature toy drum sets, a porcelain Snoopy as "Joe Writer" sitting at a typewriter, a four-inch poseable Brett Favre action figure (the one in *green* and gold, not *purple* and gold thankyouverymuch), and of course the obligatory "I luv you Dady" child art and family photos. But I'll tell you what I *don't* have displayed, and you shouldn't either:

- Those stupid-ass motivational framed prints that say "Aim High!" or "Be the Bridge!" or "Dare to Soar!" They might look nice hanging in a mahogany trimmed corporate board room, but when the shit hits the fan at work, no forced, framed phrase is going to inspire you to solve your problems and save your skin. Don't believe me? During the next office crisis, try telling your enraged boss to just "Believe and Achieve!" while pointing to your poster. Then wait for his reaction to that little pearl of wisdom.
- Cutesy animal calendars with photos of yarn-tangled kittens saying, "Try me later. I'm tied up!" or the dog with its paws over its eyes thinking, "This just isn't my day!" or the parrot

hanging upside down squawking, "Hang in there!" If you're eighty-two years old, you get a pass. Otherwise, there's simply no excuse.

- Cartoons or sarcastic signs proclaiming "The Department of I Don't Care!" or "I start working when the coffee does!" or "You're not the boss of me. My dog is!" Unless your goal is to shun colleagues and paint yourself as the ultimate poisonous employee and antiteam player who's in desperate need of an attitude adjustment, then avoid these little chestnuts. (P.S. *Dilbert* is one of the most successful syndicated comic strips in history, and I've yet to read one single strip that made me laugh. Dilbert = Don't.)

- Photos from your senior year Cancun spring break vacation. I know, drinking those body shots was the pinnacle of your social life, so naturally you want to share some photographic evidence proving you actually sucked tequila from your waitress's pierced navel. But which would you rather achieve at work: party cred or career cred? If you want to command a little respect from your colleagues between 9 A.M. and 5 P.M., then show some restraint in sharing the details of your high jinks from 5 P.M. to 9 A.M. Trust me. Your colleagues already suspected you were capable of such crass debauchery. No need to prove it to them, Stiffler.

SKIP THE INTERVIEW INTERROGATIONS

"Aren't you a little bit young for this job?"

At twenty-four, I probably was, but I got the offer anyway—despite this brazenly discriminatory question I fielded during a job interview shortly after grad school. Sure, it was all I could do to bite my tongue and not return an opposite insult, considering the interviewer at the time appeared to be pushing great-grandmother status. But looking back, that old bag's question pales in comparison to some of the more harsh interviewers out there.

You know that person who just loves playing "bad cop" when interviewing job candidates? Barely restraining himself as he strives to intimidate a candidate from across the table . . . "Do you think you can do this job better than me?" . . . "Let's cut the crap. Why do you really want to work here?" Well, when it's your turn to serve on a search committee, don't be that jerk. Unless the candidate is robotically reciting canned answers ad nauseam, have a heart and give her a break. Because when it's you who's being interviewed for a job, you'll pray that prick doesn't pick on you. And whenever you're the candidate for any job you really want, don't forget the accidental adult's Golden Rule of interviewing: Never be yourself. Instead, imitate the more mature person they'd prefer you to be—an accomplished, responsible adult.

MAINTAIN SOME PERSPECTIVE

Need a sure-fire way to tell whether a coworker is an assimilated adult or an accidental one? Use the following checklist to conduct a little informal investigation:

○ Does your coworker never miss an opportunity to participate in Secret Santa gift exchanges?

○ Does your coworker frequently leave those notes on the break room refrigerator reminding others to never take a lunch that does not belong to them?

○ Does your coworker consider it an honor, not an insult, to be named to the party-planning committee?

○ Does your coworker skip happy hour with colleagues to study up on the competition?

○ Does your coworker arrive at work exactly at 9 A.M., take exactly thirty minutes for lunch, and leave exactly at 5 P.M., every day?

If you answered yes to any of the above, you've successfully identified an assimilated adult. And if *you* are that coworker, watch out—you're becoming one of them. Some advice? Lighten up! A little flexibility and some perspective could do you some good. No one's advocating slacking off (entirely), just a slightly more relaxed attitude. Attending the occasional happy hour with your colleagues won't kill you. And if Human Resources plans an Italian-themed employee luncheon for the third year in a row, don't let their lack of creativity ruin your day. Remember, life is chock full of super-serious professional adults. We accidental adults often bring some much-needed diversity to the workplace. Corporate America: You're welcome!

ADULT APTITUDE TEST

Shortly after my teaching assistantship ended and my next job search began, my parents made one thing clear. Sitting me down in the family room beanbag chair, they told me to prepare for a work-a-day world where I'd soon end up supervising employees who are older than me and where I'd eventually acquire younger mentors who would look up to me (!) for wisdom and direction.

Of course, their prediction proved prescient. But at the time, I wasn't so sure. *A lifetime of pursuing boring adult endeavors? Just to pay the bills? Ugh. . . . Working is going to suck,* my inner smart-ass concluded.

Years later, I was only partially right. I'm still about the youngest person in the boardroom at any given time (although that's slowly starting to change), and I sometimes wear a tie just to prove I'm not the college intern. Sure, I may have matured, relented, and conformed a bit more than I'd like to admit, but I'm proud to say one thing has never gotten old along the way: my mental spirit.

Looking back on those early days, it's amazing to think I made it through that awkward transition from college to a career. I often wonder where Ed and my other students are today and if they too have finally experienced the same challenges of accidental adulthood. If they're like me, at one point or another they've likely straddled the line between the world of indoctrinated adults who have embraced life's responsibilities and the reluctant grownups who strive to remain forever young in thought and action. If I could ever catch up with my former students and deliver just one more lecture, it might sound like this:

Remember when I said maintaining eye contact was important in establishing credibility when giving a speech? Well, by now I'm sure you've discovered how critical eye contact is when also trying to fool a colleague into believing you know what you're doing. That is what they call a multipronged lesson.

Remember when I gave you two minutes to prepare an impromptu speech? Now I'll bet you wish you had that much time to pull your thoughts together whenever your boss catches you daydreaming through a meeting and surprises you with a request for your perspective on the presentation that might benefit the group. (And I'm guessing she doesn't toss you a mini Snickers bar when you're done, either.)

Remember when I asked you to always identify your sources of information to validate your claims? I pray it didn't take a humiliating boardroom argument (or the more hazardous after-work barroom altercation) to reinforce the dangers of making statements to colleagues you can't back up.

Remember when I dropped hints that my TA buddies and I would probably go out to celebrate the end of the semester before we graded your final exams? That was only to get you to find us at the bar that night and buy us drinks. Totally unprofessional. Sorry about that. Let my bad example help you to more easily spot cheap ploys for bribery like this from your supervisors in the future.

Remember when you thought I had all the answers simply because I was your teacher? Well, I'm sure by now you've figured out I didn't. And you've probably discovered by now that no one does. Not even your bosses. Sure, give them the respect they deserve, and do your best to earn some of your own. But remember, deep down ... when it comes to the workplace, we're all playing roles at times. Too often, it's the real adults who buy into their characters a little more seriously than they should, while we accidental adults strive to master the art of caring less without becoming careless. In any event, the real trick is to play your role with pride, without having the role play you.

Class dismissed. Now then ... my friends and I will be at Shooters if you'd like to stop by to just say hello.

f us never planned o

is happening. But it di

ometime between gra

chool and our first mort

age, a strange phenom

non began replacing ou

outhful mojos with

ew-found maturity. An

e didn't see it coming

ur two-door coupe

orphed into sliding

oor minivans. Bar-hop

ing turned into movi

ights on the couch. No

e write letters to th

3. MUSIC

This Is What You Call a *Mixtape*

GROWING UP IN A musical family meant a somewhat untraditional upbringing for me and my siblings (though it's not like we toured Austria singing "Edelweiss" in play clothes hand sewn from curtains). Our childhood was untraditional in the sense that most other kids our age seemed to be much more consumed with sports and outdoors activities. Instead of shanking soccer balls off goalposts in summer sports leagues like our neighbors, Megan, Ryan, and I sang and danced onstage in community college theater productions. Dinners at our house were always served with a soundtrack of the Boston Pops blasting from a boom box on the kitchen counter. And family vacations included Liberace concerts and off-Broadway touring musicals.

So by the time each of us turned nine, it came as little surprise that our parents told us we could choose any sport we wanted to play, with restrictions (noncontact sports only), and we could choose any instrument we wanted to play . . . with no restrictions.

"I'm thinking of putting the band back together. Maybe you could join us."

—Elwood Blues, *The Blues Brothers*

As an accidental adult, I've occasionally been called indecisive by my friends and family. I've been known to spend an entire weekend deciding what color shoes to buy. I once interviewed eight different friends, battering them with financial questions, before choosing a credit card with the lowest possible interest rate. But at nine years old, this musical decision that I faced—one that would ultimately prove so instrumental for me throughout my life—was the quickest decision I've ever made. It unfolded in about four minutes during a junior-high band concert one spring in the early '80s. Sitting in a sweaty gymnasium, I perched up on my folding chair craning to watch my older sister play the tenor saxophone. About midway through her jazz band's interpretation of Herbie Hancock's "Watermelon Man," a singular, transformative experience descended upon me, coming from a few rows behind my sister's woodwind section.

A drum solo.

Flailing arms . . . relentless rhythms . . . crashing cymbals . . . sixteen bars of percussive perfection. I could feel the kick of the bass drum deep in my stomach, and my eyes blinked with every crack of the snare. I was having a visceral reaction to this performance, and I loved every fleeting second of it. But the best was yet to come.

As the teenage drummer finished and the band rejoined him in song, about a half-dozen starstruck thirteen-year-old girls in the audience began to shriek wildly, calling the drummer's name. They loved the drums! They loved the solo! And most importantly, they loved him!

In that instant, my mind was made up. The French horn wasn't going to endear me to the ladies. The clarinet wasn't going to take me to the promised land either. No, I would play the drums. I would play them well. And yes, I would make girls scream.

Decades later, I'm proud to say I've fulfilled that vow *marginally* well. I've played in dance bands, jazz bands, Dixieland bands, rock bands, church groups, backyard party bands, and best of all, my college mock 'n' roll band. (We adopted our name after a class none of us ever took—Language: Power and Abuse—and branded ourselves with the world's coolest-ever slogan: "We want to work your private functions!") Along my musical journey, I've even earned an occasional cheer or two (thanks Mom and Dad!)—a far cry from a thirteen-year-old's love screech, but I'll take it.

Yet my passion for drumming and love of music has presented me with something of a dilemma these days, especially as my body ages physically while my mind seems stuck at a mental age of approximately twenty-two. And a quick survey of the reluctant grownups who surround me suggests that I am not alone.

Sooner or later, every accidental adult faces a critical decision along the journey to adulthood: Will you cling to the vestiges of your exhilarating youth or will you embrace the uncertainty of the not-so-cool future? Nothing draws this line in the sand clearer than music.

FACING THE MUSIC

Ever since the earliest days of rock 'n' roll music (think: Elvis, Jerry Lee Lewis, the Beatles), teenagers have idolized rock stars. We wanted their fame, their fortune, their groupies. A fortunate few of us could actually play an instrument well enough to form a garage band. Some of us even landed gigs that paid money or at least provided free beer. We felt the frenzy. We heard the roar of approval. We rocked and rolled and banged our heads through high school and then through college. And for those of us who didn't play an instrument, most discovered there actually was more than one way to rock (sorry Sammy). How so? I'm speaking of course about the arena rock concert, that great equalizer of musical and nonmusical youth.

For the price of a month's allowance, any angst-ridden adolescent could buy a ticket to a show and join about 20,000 other sweaty kids for a two-hour shared assault on the senses. You didn't have to be a musician. You didn't need to recognize that the guitarist was pulling off major-chord inversions. You still connected with the music and appreciated the performance. You got your money's worth when the lead singer jumped off the double bass drums as the bassist kicked over a twelve-foot stack of Marshall amps and the guitarist went into a few windmill power chords while the drummer set his gong ablaze—and meanwhile, the crowd yelled "Rock on!" with their fists in the air.

But a funny thing happened on our way to adulthood. As our twenties turned to thirties, we've become more separated from the soundtracks of our youth than we ever anticipated. Our college rock bands broke up the day we landed serious, salaried jobs. We finally can afford the price of amphitheater floor seats, but it's getting harder and harder to stand throughout entire concerts. Yet deep down we still feel that tug, that calling to reunite with our inner Bill and Ted and unleash that carefree spirit in search of a most excellent adventure.

As we reluctantly age, all of this begs the question: "When is it time to face the music?"

TRAGICALLY HIP OR JUST TRAGIC?

You tell me what's sadder: announcing to friends that you're getting the band back together or actually doing it? When is it no longer cool to thrust up the heavy metal horn hand salute and yell out song requests at a rock concert? And what the hell does a suburban parent of three wear to a rock concert these days anyway?

All of these questions deserve some answers, because when it comes to music, many accidental adults feel like solo acts. Clearly there's a fine line between becoming tragically hip and just plain tragic, and on any given day, I precariously straddle that edge. So for my sake as well as yours, let's review a few helpful hints together from . . .

THE MUSIC LOVER'S GUIDE TO ACTING YOUR AGE WITHOUT LOSING YOUR COOL

GETTING THE BAND BACK TOGETHER

So it's been fourteen years since you and your college buddies last played a sloppy power chord together. Thinking about entering a battle of the bands competition that features the freshest young talent around? Think again. Considering a gig at the local community center band shell? Reconsider. There are fewer sights sadder than aging amateur rock bands that take themselves too seriously while playing to eye-rolling and head-scratching onlookers. Save your tongue-in-cheek antics for the backyard party, where your audience featuring a few dozen friends will get the joke.

BRAGGING ABOUT THE GLORY DAYS

You used to play in a band? That's great! Now shut the hell up. We've all been stuck in a corner with this guy, and when we do, we usually give our spouse the "save me from this conversation" signal. It usually goes like this. "Yeah, I was in a band once. Damn near made it big time. Nearly snagged a recording contract. Had a pretty good following for a while there. . . ." Usually unprompted bravado like this is directed toward women in a desperate attempt to get lucky.

But I can pretty much guarantee you that in the recorded annals of history, talk like this has never gotten that guy laid. So keep it to yourself, Ace. It wasn't going to happen anyway.

GUITAR ZEROS

Never fall victim to the intoxicating delusion that proficiency at Guitar Hero could translate into actual musical acumen. If you'd like to earn a reputation as a guitar god, here's a suggestion: Stop playing video games and learn how to play an actual guitar.

RATING RADIO

Don't be that douchebag who swears he hasn't listened to the radio in ten years 'cause it all sucks now. Or the equally insufferable jackass who claims the only good music came off those obscure early albums before the artist "sold out to the man" and started churning out radio-ready commercial hits. Wait a minute . . . that douchebag sounds a lot like me! I'd better reread my own advice here. . . .

AIR DRUMMING

Don't do it. Well, unless it's along with Phil Collins's signature "In the Air Tonight" drum entrance. Wait, that's cheesy, too. Nope. No air drumming. Ever.

SPENDING MONEY ON MUSIC

After spending $250 on a ticket to the Police reunion concert, I won't be winning the Frugal Father of the Year award anytime soon. Was it the wisest financial move for a father of three small, needy kids to make? Probably not. Did it drain my children's college savings accounts? Not exactly (considering I don't have such accounts). Did I joy cry a little when they opened with "Message in a Bottle?" What do you think? So don't beat yourself up over a few pricey tickets, especially if the show is a once-in-a-lifetime event. And if you can't intercept the credit card statement from the mailbox, simply remind your shell-shocked wife that supporting the arts is always a generous move. (Very adultlike, too!)

YOU JUST *HAVE* TO LISTEN TO THIS!

Whatever music you choose to purchase, enjoy it solo and don't force it on others. Making mix tapes and burning best-of CDs was a great way to nurture a crush when you were younger, but today, no one needs to hear early INXS blasting from the bowels of your Toyota Camry. Why? Few people care what music you like, and no one wants to hear you explain that you only listen to old INXS because they went all "dance club" on you with the *Kick* album.

CONCERT ETIQUETTE

Back in the day, no one had to tell you how to behave at a rock concert. But now that you're on the cusp of becoming culturally irrelevant, you probably can use a tip or two for navigating the ins and outs of an arena show. So before you go "kicking it with the kids," consider a few of these questions first.

What to Wear?

You're years out of college and its dress code of hip-high denim. But you're also decades away from the retirement home and its days of nipple-high polyester pants. So what's an accidental adult supposed to wear to a rock concert?

Ladies: If you're going to commit a fashion faux pas, a rock concert is the place to do it. So, is this the time and the place to "go ho?" Well, there are relatively few other public venues where society will give you such a free pass. So if you're going to make a mistake, err on the side of saucy. I'm not suggesting you go for hooker chic, or revisit the days of plunging neck lines, black leather miniskirts, and high heel boots (although I probably won't argue with that call). I'm just saying to at least leave those elastic-waist, pleated "Mom jeans" at home and slip into those low-rise denims instead. Top it off with a black belly shirt and you'll pass muster with the men, especially with clueless, intoxicated friends like mine.

Guys: I really don't care what you wear to a concert. Unless during my search to admire a few low-rise jeans and black belly shirts I spot you . . . wearing low-rise jeans and a black belly shirt.

When to Arrive?

In younger years, you probably showed up in time to catch the opening act on the chance that you'd catch a rising star, and because you had plenty of time on your hands and enough stamina to stand around for hours. Now that you're older, you've realized life is too short to waste on warm-up bands. Ask the bartender to pour you another pint before you head across the street to the concert hall. Then nurse that beer from the comforts of a barstool until the roadies are clearing off the opening band's gear because your lower back is in for one hell of a night.

Sit or Stand?

At twenty-two years old, sitting wasn't even a consideration—unless your girlfriend dragged you to an Indigo Girls concert and a chair offered you your only reprieve from public humiliation and disgrace. But by thirty-two, standing for more than two hours straight becomes a painful proposition. Thank God for the guitar solo. Or the drum solo. Or even more rare (but especially restful), the bass solo. These moments of ostentatious rock-star self-indulgence provide any accidental adult the relief necessary to withstand the rest of the show atop a pair of sensible orthopedic Oxfords.

What to Drink (and How Much)?

This really shouldn't be a question. Yet sadly, here we are because of guys like my friend Brian, who downed four hard lemonades just seven songs into the Van Halen reunion concert. His embarrassing beverage of choice in this particular venue was roughly the equivalent to drinking wine coolers at a monster truck show. It's pretty simple really. Rock concerts equals beer only. And slow down! What makes you think that the same prostate problem that keeps you stumbling to the toilet in the middle of the night is going to miraculously correct itself at a concert? Drinking in moderation will keep your bathroom breaks to a minimum so you can avoid those long lines to the urinals that take shape during the Keith Richards set.

Be Yourself or Blend In?

Let's keep the spotlight on the stage, not on the aging loser wearing his tie around his forehead. You might be an accidental adult, but you're technically still an adult. This means no moshing, no yelling

"Free Bird!," no hoisting your girlfriend onto your shoulders, and no making out during power ballads. Feeling your age a bit too much? Don't go too far in the other direction, either. This means no leaving the arena before the encore just so you can beat traffic home. And if you smell weed wafting down from the rafters, don't call for security like you did on those punks hanging out under the bleachers at your local high school's Homecoming football game. You may be decades apart from those guys, but for one night only, you're supposed to be on the same team . . . Team Rock!

The Concert Tee?

Go ahead. Buy one. And then roll that sandpaper-soft Beefy-T into a ball and stuff it in the back of your closet for good. When you discover it during Goodwill donation time, you can wistfully stare at it and remember the night you spent $40 for a 75¢ shirt you never wore.

MAKE A LOUD MISTAKE

There will always be a special place in my heart for musicians and music lovers alike, no matter how many of these guidelines they ignore as they indulge in their passion for music. Anyone who knows the true backstory to U2's "Sunday Bloody Sunday" is as sharp as any history scholar in my book. Any singer who can spew by memory the speed lyrics of REM's "It's the End of the World as We Know It" deserves a high-five, all the way up (and I'll feel fine). And any DJ who refuses to cut off the original extended version ending of Prince's "Purple Rain" (so I can pull over in my car and sway my arms back and forth above my head, singing, "Woo-hoo-hoo-hoo

. . . Woo-hoo-hoo-hoo"), well . . . I would . . . die 4 . . . U. Trouble is, as we get older, I'm seeing more and more adults who'd like to rock out but won't. They've forgotten the thrill of eardrum-shattering concerts and would rather read the concert review in the morning paper instead. They're turning their radio dials away from their kid's pop rock or hip-hop stations and locking into adult contemporary or easy listening stations, just to find comfort and familiarity. And worst of all, I hear many former musicians say they're reluctant to dust off their guitars and power up their amps for fear of looking like clueless Spinal Tappers.

In a ridiculous world where the Police is now considered classic rock, I can't say I blame you for feeling a tad lost. But let me offer you a bit of advice I got from my first drum teacher. After hearing me butcher Van Halen's frenetically syncopated "Everybody Wants Some" for the eleventh time, he noticed I was becoming increasingly timid and hesitant. He told me to play out, and that if I were going to make a mistake, I should always make it a loud one.

On that note, I offer this: For those about to rock, I really do salute you. A heavy metal horn salute, that is, with a head bang and a "Rock on!" to boot. And if you're going to make a mistake or two in your journey through adulthood, make them unabashedly loud as well. Life as an accidental adult means you will make plenty of loud mistakes on your multicity world tour. A few blunders will strike the wrong chord with some people. But more often than not you'll find the assimilated adult society will consider most of your mistakes very forgivable and often quite charming as long as you're marching to the beat of your own drummer.

f us never planned o
his happening. But it di
ometime between gra
chool and our first mort
age, a strange phenom
non began replacing ou
outhful mojos with
ew-found maturity. An
e didn't see it coming
ur two-door coupe
morphed into sliding
oor minivans. Bar-hop
ing turned into movi
ights on the couch. No
e write letters to th
ditor. And golfe. It's

4. SUBURBIA

Keeping Your Poise 'n the Hood

"WE'RE GOING TO DIE in this house." If that sounds like a line from a horror film, you're not too far off. Sure, I was dramatic issuing this decree to Kelly when we moved into our current house. But this was our third move in eight years, and I wanted it to be our last. A marriage can be a fragile enough venture without the pressures of buying and selling multiple properties so often. And it didn't help matters that throughout most of our moves I relegated most of the heavy lifting to my wife—much like any irresponsible accidental adult would do. Finding a successful Realtor? I trust Kelly's instincts. Deciphering mortgage options? She's better at math. Researching title companies? Just tell me when it's over.

Despite my lack of participation in sorting out many of these mind-numbing details, I did eventually grow a pair when I took the lead on the most humbling experience involved in the entire real estate process: the inspection. This is the day when a home expert explains the difference between wood

"It's one hell of a day in my neighborhood, a hell of a day for a neighbor."

—"Mister Robinson's Neighborhood," *Saturday Night Live*

clapboard siding and pressed wood fiber hardboard siding while accidental adults like me nod incessantly to feign comprehension. We even have a video that Kelly shot of me following the inspector around the house like a lost puppy, taking notes on a clipboard (no idea what I was writing), and scratching my head a lot.

Looking back on our latest (and final) move, I think both Kelly and I may have missed the most important step of this monumental transaction. Sure, that home inspection was vitally important, but what was really much more necessary was a thorough neighborhood inspection. Before we moved in, we knew our prospective neighborhood featured most of the basic prerequisites important to any young couple looking to raise a family—topnotch schools, nearby parks and trails, well-kempt lawns, and other families with young children. But if conducted properly, a more complete investigation would have featured a checklist that looked something like this:

Ideal Accidental Adult Neighborhood

- ☑ Garages filled to the rafters with multiple tool storage systems ready to serve as your own private (and free) rental center.
- ☑ Fences, tall hedges, or other visual barriers that conceal your botched backyard landscaping projects.
- ☑ Endless supplies of free firewood someone else cut and stored in the woods behind your house. (That's communal, right?)
- ☑ Front porches decorated with enough wind chimes to effectively drown out your wife's voice as she berates you from open windows during summer months.
- ☑ MILFs

In my book, if a neighborhood can offer any of those amenities, I simply ask, would you be mine? Could you be mine? Won't you be my *neighbor*hood? Because guys like me who have no right living among the grownups deserve a homebound haven where we can seek refuge from the adult responsibilities of the real world and do things our way—the wrong way. A place where we can accidentally spill 10W-30 down our driveways while changing our lawn mower oil. A place where we can behead a garter snake with a dull shovel because it surprised the shit out of us, and now the sneaky bastard simply deserves to die. A place where we can put our four-year-old daughters on the back of a motor scooter for a quick zip across the front lawn (at slow speeds, Kelly). A place where we can do all of these things—without the prying eyes of scoffing, pedantic neighbors.

Fortunately, Kelly and I lucked out by moving into a wonderful development full of highly supportive neighbors who are no more judgmental than are we. In the process, I discovered that finding a fantastic 'hood like ours is key to the psychological and sociological well-being of any accidental adult. Because like it or not, where you live often becomes the interrogation room for adult-aptitude assessments—the place where others will perform daily evaluations of your skills and qualifications as an adult.

You might think you've mastered more challenging performance appraisals elsewhere, but I doubt it. At work, you probably perform your role as diligently as any actor would, thinking before you speak, pausing before you act. And in public places like churches, restaurants, and shopping malls, you're on your best behavior, demonstrating patience with your loving spouse and the (obnoxious) strangers around you. But at home? Well, few of us accidental adults have the stamina to maintain the charade of conformity to the adult world around the clock. So home is where you let it all hang out, demonstrating that the True You is the Home You, not the Work You or the Public You. Nope, the Home You tells the world just exactly what kind of backwards-ass poseur you really can be (most days of the week). So if all the world's a stage, then choosing your neighborhood is a bit like picking the platform upon which a white hot spotlight will follow your every move. Choose wisely and your audience's empathy could elevate your performance. Make a rash decision and look out for flying tomatoes.

ENTER . . . APATHY

Remember those idyllic Norman Rockwell days of your youth, when your mother sent you across the street to borrow a cup of sugar from your neighbors so she could finish baking you a chocolate cake? Those childhood memories all came flooding back to me one Sunday not long ago when liquor stores were closed and we realized we were out of wine. So we sent our nine-year-old daughter down the street to a neighbor's house with a Rubbermaid water bottle for them to fill. Fortunately for us, no one called Child Protective Services to intercept her as she skipped back down the block to us, carrying a transparent bottle filled with red alcohol.

Now believe it or not, this fleeting moment of bad parenting actually represented a symbolic victory to us for two reasons. First, we weren't alone in exercising poor judgment because this favor required two other supposed adults to comply with our request to give our young daughter alcohol to carry home to us. What luck! If there's anything an accidental adult loves it's company. And secondly, this incident exemplified a breakthrough into the wonderful world of apathetic adulthood, and it was a well-deserved breakthrough at that. After decades of caring a little too much about what others thought about us, Kelly and I learned that sometimes (just sometimes) caring about image isn't always worth the energy.

When you're trying to keep up appearances with the Joneses in surburbia, you have to be careful. Sure, there is some freedom in the

Rockwell landscape—and opportunities for you to avoid the prim and proper—but never forget you are on their turf.

EVENTUALLY . . . ADAPTATION

Despite my unrealized childhood dream of escaping the fishbowl of my small town and carving out a lively metropolitan life, I've eventually adjusted to a much more subdued, if not surveyed, existence in suburbia instead. In fact, it's come to suit me well—primarily because I've learned to adapt to my environment and to take the accidental adult's "I don't give a damn" attitude. Then I balance that 'tude with the necessary need to conform just enough to placate the assimilated adults and occasionally resemble a responsible neighbor. See, each of my postcollege residences has taught me that every suburban neighborhood has its own set of social mores. Some are spoken, but most are simply understood. And like it or not, it's your responsibility as the so-called adult to decipher this code of responsible and courteous neighborly conduct if you truly want to blend into the woodwork of the white picket fences. Of course, depending on where you live, your rules for a mature, neighborly coexistence might differ slightly. But you can find a universal nugget of wisdom or two in my list of . . .

UNNATURAL BUT NEIGHBORLY GESTURES THAT ADULTS SEEM TO APPRECIATE

DON'T SET YOUR GARBAGE CANS OUT ON THE DRIVEWAY THE NIGHT BEFORE PICKUP

In the first few weeks in my newfound suburbia, I thought I was demonstrating remarkable maturity and uncharacteristic proactivity by dragging my trash to the curb the night before the trucks rolled through the development. But as one neighbor told me, "It kind of shits up the neighborhood having the trash out on your driveway any minute longer than necessary." If I recall, my inspired reply was, "Oh," and ever since, I've wheeled my garbage and recycling cans out in the cruel wee hours of the morning. If your neighborhood's sentiment on early trash storage is like mine, the good news is they care. The bad news is they probably care just a little too much. My advice? Follow their lead, muffle your grumbles, and transport your trash to the curb in the morning, when you're likely in a bad mood anyway.

CONSIDER YOUR NEIGHBOR'S PRIDE
BEFORE DOING HIM A FAVOR

The best $100 I ever spent was on a used snowblower I purchased from a garage sale in preparation for my first winter as a new homeowner. At age twenty-six, I considered this glorious electric-start Toro a fascinating new toy required of all soon-to-be adults. But that winter, in my hasty exuberance to fire up that beautiful single-stage engine and keep it running, I assumed that my overworked police officer neighbor wouldn't mind (and might even appreciate it) if I walked across the street and plowed out his driveway after I finished my own. After clearing about half of his driveway, I looked up to see him stumbling out his side door, throwing on his parka, and trudging toward me with a look on his face that said, "Thanks for dragging my ass out of bed on my day off so I could relieve *you* from doing *my* job on *your* schedule." I could picture his wife minutes earlier shouting at him inside, "Honey, that poor skinny Colin is out there snowblowing our driveway! What's the matter with you? Get out there!"

Since then I have come to realize that in a real adult's world (not mine) there is something emasculating about another man snowblowing your driveway. It's viewed as a sign of weakness, a vulnerability, an indicator of incompetence. If you're a neighbor of mine, understand that I do not share this viewpoint, and please consider yourself more than welcome to lend me a hand. But if you're the average adult, take this perspective into consideration before you decide to help a brother out without an invitation. One man's favor is another's disgrace. To sidestep this awkward dance, consider calling your neighbor before performing your random (but invasive) act of kindness. You might even save a marriage in the process, at least for one cold morning.

BOO WHO? START A NEW HOLIDAY
TRADITION INSTEAD

If you need any evidence that society's respect for personal boundaries has evaporated, I would point you to the increasingly popular neighborhood tradition of "BOOing" your neighbors. If this bit of forced fun hasn't yet arrived in your part of suburbia, let me explain how it works in mine.

Sometime in mid-October, just as you're sitting down to enjoy a rare warm dinner with your family, your doorbell rings. When you open the front door to greet this untimely caller, the only thing visible on your doorstep is a bag of treats with a letter informing your kids (to their delight and your dismay), "You've been BOOed!" Typically the goody bag only contains chocolate for the kids, but if you're lucky, your neighbor might include a can of beer or two for you. If only the merriment could stop here. Nope. This care package also includes a corny poem and detailed instructions pressuring you to participate in this glorified chain letter by repeating this secret gesture for two or three neighbors of your choice. It's a subtle demand to scrounge around your cupboards to assemble a creative collection of treats in the name of bringing some "ghostly cheer" to "neighbors far or near." And as if once a year wasn't enough, a mere two months later this tradition inexplicably returns, having now morphed into its Christmas counterpart, "You've been jingled!"

I realize I may sound like a Scrooge (or his curmudgeonly Halloween counterpart), but the burdensome pressure I feel to keep this game going trounces the momentary thrill. Granted, today's BOO-ing is probably payback for my childhood's Ding-Dong-Ditch prank (except there's no bag of flaming dog poop to extinguish on your welcome mat). Yet there's something about BOOing that feels a bit too invasive to me.

When the BOOing begins, you really have little choice but to play along, otherwise you risk earning a reputation as the neighborhood buzz killer. But if surprises with sweets is the way your neighborhood rolls, then why not take the treating tradition in another direction, a path that allows you to reap the fullest recognition your selfless efforts in the kitchen truly deserve? St. Patrick's Day is a big deal in our household and an often overlooked holiday after graduating beyond the college bar scene. So I decided years ago to seize that day to repay my neighborhood for its year-round kindnesses. My solution? Shamrock-shaped green JELL-O jigglers created with the help of my own three leprechauns. And by hand delivering the gelatin treats door-to-door in the morning, I get the praise and appreciation that eludes those anonymous nighttime BOOers.

So pick an available holiday in need of attention and make it your own. Knock out your neighbors with a box cake on Boxing Day. Roll out some homemade egg rolls for Chinese New Year. Or bring them a boat load of biscotti for Columbus Day. Just remember—sometimes it's not your thought that counts. It's the thoughtfulness of your generosity without the expectation of participation or reciprocation that matters a lot, too.

KEEP YOUR POLITICAL OPINIONS TO YOURSELF

If you're lucky, maybe once or twice in your life you will find a political candidate who really represents your beliefs. The kind of person who makes you think, "This guy is just like me, but without a stunted maturity crippling his ability to actually make things happen." And when that candidate comes along, your knee-jerk reaction might be to shout your allegiance over hill, over dale. But there's no quicker way to alienate yourself from your neighbors than forcing them to look at a political yard sign on your front lawn for three months—especially if "your guy" isn't "their guy." And if your 'hood is like mine, you'll have a better chance of getting your neighbors to approve a hazardous waste site at the end of your street than to support your candidate. So since you're not likely to sway opinions and move the mass electorate with a 12" x 24" piece of corrugated plastic rising from your grass, why go there? Your neighbors may have the maturity to handle a little silent dissonance without making an obvious fuss, but I guarantee you your yard sign will endure months of mental egging.

DON'T BE A CHICKEN, CROSS THE ROAD

Most of us have that neighbor who will gladly interrupt his outdoor project, lean against a shovel, and shoot the shit with anyone who walks by his front lawn. This is also the same guy who stocks his garage refrigerator with cases of Miller High Life (the champagne of beer) and routinely hosts impromptu thirty-minute garage conversations leaning against his SUV or his pickup with anyone who will join him for a cold one.

Well, I happen to have about twelve of these guys on my street. Each one is a hell of a guy whose company I genuinely enjoy, and there are plenty of days when I wish I could be more like them. Sometimes I even think, "Why not check in? See what's new? Stop for a minute and catch up?" But invariably I then remember that I have a lawn to mow, rain gutters to clear, and my wife's expecting the garage to be clean by the time she gets home. The result? I usually offer the obligatory wave before returning to my busy work, or I become a bit too jumpy closing the garage door mere seconds after I pull my car inside.

My 100 percent Polish father had the patience of a saint. My 100 percent Irish mother, not so much. So I believe her when she tells me I get my severe impatience from her. Even though she chooses to find its genetic roots charming, my lack of patience coupled with my increasing introversion (not to mention an aversion to distractions) forms a deadly combination that could be misinterpreted by my neighbors as aloofness instead of more accurately reflecting the telltale signs of accidental adulthood. Ironically, no one feels less superior to his neighbors than I do. That's why I've found it helpful to occasionally tell them so. I've found that when you're not the chattiest guy on the block, it never hurts to tell your neighbors "It's not you, it's me," so as to prevent acquiring an antisocial reputation. It also helps to throw them a bone every once in a while and force an over-the-hedge conversation during those rare backyard moments when you're not on the clock.

Yes, ideally you'd like to avoid exposure as a fraud by limiting all conversations to less than two minutes anytime you find yourself among real adults in your neighborhood. Nothing particularly productive or revelatory comes out of these interactions. But it does help to occasionally put the rake down, cross the street, and join the club—just to demonstrate that when push comes to shove, you really are one of them, even though you aren't.

MAINTAIN CURB APPEAL
(FOR YOUR NEIGHBORS—NOT FOR YOU)

I know plenty of people who honestly believe that the most attractive house on their block should be their own. Really? How often do you sit back to admire your own home's exterior aesthetics? You can't do that too well looking out your front window can you? The house that really matters is the one *you* have to look at. And it's located directly across the street. In a perfect world, we'd all get to beautify our neighbor's house and vice versa. Imagine the joy of spending their money while you pick out your neighbor's exterior siding color, or choose their roofing tiles, or select and position their newly planted trees and shrubbery. Until that glorious day arrives, I suppose we all should apply the Golden Rule with our own curb appeal efforts. That means doing unto our houses (within a limited budget) what we wish our neighbors would do unto their houses (sky's the limit, Rockefellers!).

AND FINALLY . . . ASSIMILATION

If any of those considerate deeds feel forced, awkward, or a tad too token, then allow me to say, "Welcome to the neighborhood!" Because believe me, I feel your pain. I've spent far too many days fighting conformity before I realized that assimilating into suburbia becomes inevitable. Before you know it, you'll be monitoring speeders who cruise through the cul-de-sac and barking at those teenagers with an effortless irritability typically displayed by only the grouchiest of adults. And soon enough, you'll find yourself spending the better part of a lazy afternoon gazing out the window from the comforts of your favorite recliner watching an albino squirrel scurry around your yard, nibbling on the pretzel log you jammed into the ground for it.

That's not to say you won't be bewildered and dismayed at times when this metamorphosis from detached observer to sometimes attentive suburban adult occurs. It's a sad progression indeed. Yet there are plenty of reasons to remain positive. If you make the choice to live in a friendly, supportive, and occasionally inquisitive suburb like mine, you sometimes need to sift the inherent benefits from the inevitable drawbacks. When you do, I hope you discover your patch of suburbia is a lot like mine in these ways:

- You might feel your movements are overly monitored at times, with little room to make schedule variations without causing alarm. But it's also a helpful place where your neighbors will alert you when you've left your garage door open after 10 P.M. or if they've noticed you've left your outdoor floodlights turned on for three consecutive nights (and ask if you're okay).
- You might feel overloaded watching your neighbors' kids on top of looking after your own. But it's also a supportive place where you can call any of a handful of neighbors for emergency childcare help whenever you're running late and you can't make it home in time to meet your kids off the school bus.
- You might feel overmatched by more responsible, capable adults who always seem to execute home improvement projects with precision, care, and ease. But it's also a generous place where those same adults are always willing to power down their lawn edgers and help you figure out how to start yours (even though it *has* to be a deficiency within the tool itself).
- You might occasionally feel antisocial in comparison to your circle of neighborhood friends who continue to party long after

you left the dinner party, mentally exhausted by 11 P.M. But it's those same special, close, and cherished relationships you have built over time that have also created that utopian place where you can sponge alcohol from them—free of judgment and free of replacement—whenever you're desperately in need.

We all deserve that beautiful day in the neighborhood—a beautiful day for a neighbor—especially if you're an accidental adult. But you don't have to hop on Mister Rogers' trolley to the Neighborhood of Make-Believe to find it. Instead, take the time to make certain your new property is accidental adult friendly before you sign any purchase agreement. If you're like me, it may take a few marriage-testing moves before you settle into your final resting place, and even then you'll sometimes feel like the little kid who got invited to sit at the adults' table on Thanksgiving.

So for your sanity and your family's, try to maintain some perspective throughout the natural ups and downs that are intrinsic to suburbia. There's a reason the grass is always greener on the other side of the fence, and it usually has something to do with your neighbor's in-ground irrigation system that's vastly superior to yours. But remember, if there's any justice in this adult-centric world, the water bill is higher over there, too.

f us never planned o
his happening. But it di
ometime between gra
chool and our first mort
age, a strange phenom
non began replacing ou
outhful mojos with
ew-found maturity. An
e didn't see it coming
ur two-door coupe
orphed into sliding
oor minivans. Bar-hop
ng turned into movi
ights on the couch. No
e write letters to th
ditor. And golfs. It's

5. ENTERTAINING

WTF? (Why Three Forks?)

ONE SATURDAY NOT LONG ago, I got a call from my friend James, who was preparing to host his annual chili cook-off party.

"Colin, I'm at the liquor store, and I think I should buy some wine for tonight," he explained. "I mean, I'm not going to drink any, but I think I should have some there, right?"

"Yeah, I guess."

"So what are some names of, like, the red wines? 'Cause that goes with chili and stuff, right?"

I thought James was smarter than this. Not that I expected him to know about wine, but that he placed his faith in me to provide an intelligent answer.

"You realize this is like the blind leading the blind," I replied.

"Hey! How come my plate's less fancy than everyone else's? Do you not trust me with a fancy plate?"

—Joey Tribbiani, *Friends*

EMILY POST VERSUS WEINER ROAST

Nothing separates the real adults from the accidental adults quite like entertaining. An assimilated adult probably knows his cabs from his Chiantis. But not us. In fact, when it comes to entertaining or simply being entertained, we accidental adults look remarkably alike. Recognize any of these telltale traits?

- ☑ Your most cherished drinking glasses have logos or slogans on them.
- ☑ At dinner parties, you repeatedly check your watch because it's approaching eight o'clock and the hostess hasn't served the main course yet.
- ☑ You don't know how to valet.
- ☑ You stammer when the bartender asks you what kind of gin you'd prefer in your martini. (*Note: He wasn't being considerate. That asshole simply wanted to bust you for ordering outside of your light beer comfort zone.*)
- ☑ You never open bottles of wine or champagne in front of others because you're certain you'll chew up the wine cork, and the sound of a champagne cork popping kind of scares you.

Trouble is, as we get older, the world of entertaining and socializing is virtually unavoidable. Yet parties now painfully illustrate one of life's most awkward transitions—a journey from balls-out, go-for-broke revelry to responsible, restrained, and refined celebration. Back in the day, you loved meeting strangers at a party. These days your excuse for skipping a get-together with a new crowd of people is because you have plenty of friends already. You used to drink fast and furiously to get the quickest jolt possible and then performed masterful buzz maintenance throughout the night. Now you drink early and quit early so you can be sober by the time you have to drive the babysitter home. It used to be socially acceptable (and fiscally necessary) to itemize your own meal off the table's multiple-party bill. Lately you hardly bat an eye when someone suggests splitting the bill four ways, even if you ordered the pasta and your friends had the prime rib.

Sure you're reluctantly maturing (read: becoming less fun). And by now you may even know which fork to use with your salad. But deep down you still feel out of place in the world of hospitality.

So how does an accidental adult properly party with professional adults who have graduated beyond Jäger shots and keggers?

I say forget about Emily Post's etiquette and instead allow me to offer you a few tips for navigating a handful of the most common festivities you'll encounter along your reluctant journey to adulthood. Who knows? You might even end up becoming the life of the party—without having to put a lampshade on your head. Let's party.

HALLOWEEN

When I was in college, there were two things I could be counted on doing every fall for which I would be mercilessly teased the rest of the semester:

1. I would dress as a pirate every Halloween.
2. I would get my hair permed every Thanksgiving break.

No matter how hard I defended my wavy mullet, I never convinced my friends it was acceptable. I get it now—if a guy has curly hair, girls expect it be natural, and real men simply don't put curlers in their hair. But to this day, I fail to see what was so taboo about pretending to be a kick-ass, rock 'n' roll pirate. I mean, compare this costume choice to my friend Brian's ill-advised outfit our sophomore year. That year he decided to break the cardinal rule of Halloween costumes for college students everywhere: "Try to look hot so you can get some." What was his misguided mistake? Brian chose to impersonate our residence hall director, who happened to be a menopausal woman in her midfifties. Okay, maybe girls don't swoon over wannabe swashbucklers, but what coed wants to make out with a guy wearing lipstick, a stuffed bra, a dress, and a powder-white wig? (No surprise to anyone, except him, Brian slept alone that night.)

Every year this daunting holiday grows more and more popular. And as it expands, I become more and more bewildered. It used to be enough to dress up your kids and send them out for a night of trick-or-treating and frightful fun. Now, as if they've been cheated somehow, adults have to get in on the action, decorating their homes and throwing the increasingly uncomfortable adult Halloween costume party.

You might think that reluctant grownups would relish the opportunity to wear a disguise, since they often feel like they're masquerading through the adult world anyway. But not this accidental adult. To be honest, adults who wear costumes kind of freak me out. And it's largely because I never know how an adult is supposed to react to this charade. Do you laugh at the Amish farmer, or is that politically incorrect? Do you compliment the Geisha girl for a historically accurate outfit, or does that say you know a little too much about Asia's personal entertainers? Do you blatantly ignore the guy in the *Friday the 13th* "Jason" hockey mask who's desperately trying to get your attention—unless he identifies himself? (*Yes!*)

Chances are, you're going to experience this cast of characters and more at your next adult costume party. Sadly, my firsthand experience with these clowns qualifies me to offer a few coping mechanisms for your close encounters of the creepy kind.

The Sports Jersey Guy

Now here's a guy who deserves your respect, so give it up for him. His lack of creativity clearly demonstrates he's been goaded into throwing together a last-minute costume for a party he probably didn't want to attend in the first place. Nicely done number 12! And thanks for leaving the number 69 jersey at home. Same with your "UMass Debate" college T-shirt. Would love to see your closet someday.

The French Maid/Sexy Black Cat/Scantily Clad Cavewoman

Take your pick, but all of these costumes scream, "It's okay to ogle me. Really, I want you to." But do not fall for this trap. Instead, consider a pre-emptive strike. Before your wife mentions anything on the car ride home, ask her, "Did you see that slut in the Playboy Bunny outfit?" You'll get honesty points for acknowledging the obvious, plus extra credit for calling that suggestive attention-seeker a skank.

The Mobster

That violin case? His daughter's. The white fedora? His grandfather's. The double-breasted pinstripe suit? His. And there's the true crime. Politely invite him to join you at the next Men's Wearhouse two-for-one suit sale. If he's smart, that's an offer he won't refuse.

The '60s Girl

Considering she wasn't alive during this decade, you can understand her fascination with the 1960s—and her confusion in putting together the right costume. Some choose the flower power hippie look, with the smoked sunglasses, flaired long sleeves, and matching bell-bottom jeans. Then there's the go-go dancer guise with the miniskirt and the knee-high white leather boots. Flash this one the peace sign for deciding to go-go shag-a-delic, baby.

The Pimp

This is the guy who takes his velvet purple suit and big daddy cane a tad too seriously and decides tonight's the night to show off his acting chops. So Mr. Method Actor usually can be found throwing out awkward and uncomfortable insults or pickup lines to the Naughty Nurse "because it's all part of the act, *beeatch*." I know it's tempting to come to her rescue, but let it go. Only an assimilated adult would think now's the time to give this asshole a lecture on the traumatic psychological affects of sexual enslavement. It's the true accidental adult who realizes that anyone who wears a candy striper dress with white fishnet stockings to a Halloween party probably knows how to put a pimp in his place anyway.

The Toga Guy

In terms of simplicity, this is one notch above a white-sheeted ghost costume. For originality, this is one step below a witch. But give the guy credit for giving it the old college try. Back in the day, Roman senators probably got way more action than permed pirates did, so who am I to judge?

– – –

If you've had enough of your ghoulish get-together and you want to clear the party early, quietly make friends with the fog machine. When no one's looking, set it to "high" mode or simply slip some chunks of dry ice into the punch bowl. Either move will bring the guests to the brink of asphyxiation. With a little luck, carbon dioxide can really change the chemistry of your next costume party, and shorten its duration considerably.

CHRISTMAS PARTIES

Every December, I spend the better part of one Saturday baking a dozen loaves of pumpkin bread and freezing them to later give as hostess gifts when attending a slew of holiday parties. And every year, like clockwork, Kelly enters the kitchen exactly halfway through this laborious process and asks me why I can't keep the counters clean. I consider this a bit like telling a heart surgeon who's halfway through surgery that the operating table is a little bit bloody right now. Really, what does it matter, as long as a temporary disaster gets tidied up in the end?

So why do I put up with this seasonal mess? Two reasons. First, I'm secure enough in my quasi-masculinity to admit I kind of enjoy baking. Second, I've yet to find a more creative gift idea than giving pumpkin bread to the people who seem obligated to include me in their Christmas celebrations every year.

These days everyone rants about the overcommercialization of Christmas. Of course their complaints are justifiable, but I'm much more annoyed by the overcelebration of Christmas. Specifically, I mean the work party, the spouse's work party, the neighborhood party, the college friend's party, the family party, the church volunteer party . . . I know *you* get the point. It's the real adults who don't have a clue.

Most accidental adults aren't opposed to partying. It's just that when the celebrations become never-ending, the chances you'll be exposed as a grown-up fraud become seemingly infinite as well.

So if endless partying is not the reason for your season, you'll tire of the Yuletide in a hurry. No worries, though. Here are twelve ways to make the twelve days of Christmas a much more entertaining time of year for your most important loved one: you!

1. Secret Santas

For most accidental adults, there's a limit to the energy and creativity it takes to think of original gift ideas. Ideally these efforts should be channeled toward the people with whom you share a home, not a break room. In a perfect world, the stale office tradition of Secret Santa gift-giving would be optional. But if you can't avoid this ritual, keep your gifts appropriately clean and inoffensive. There's nothing funny about a harassment complaint filed in your name with Human Resources, especially during the holidays.

2. Egg Nog

If you're like me, you should say no to the nog, unless you want a 3 A.M. reminder of everything you ate at the party. What genius thought mixing milk with raw eggs and liquor was a good idea?

3. Kissing under the Mistletoe

Don't try it, unless tricking others into awkward and uncomfortable sexual advances is your thing. Then who am I to judge?

4. Removing Your Shoes

Here's the holiday party where half the guests hobble around cold kitchen floors in their socks all night, glaring at the other guests who didn't offer to take off their shoes at the door. In my experience, the majority of the shoeless guests would gladly pass the hat and contribute to a carpet-cleaning fund in exchange for the privilege to wear their shoes (especially women who largely seem to think shoes are the most important accessory to their outfit). To avoid going shoeless, do your best to create a distraction when entering the home so your hostess won't have an opportunity to explain her rules for keeping her carpets clean. A quick dash to the bathroom with an "I'm breaking the seal!" explanation usually suffices.

5. P.C. or Not P.C.?

For Christ's sake, it's Christmas! So why not say so? Can't you just smell the fear every time you hear people wishing each other a politically correct "Happy Holidays" instead of a "Merry Christmas"? I figure if a Jewish Neil Diamond can record one of the coolest Christmas albums ever produced, this gives us all the right to say "Merry Christmas" regardless of religion.

6. Decorations

This one's really, really simple yet so often ignored. Your house's outdoor Christmas decorations go up no sooner than Thanksgiving Day, and they come down no later than New Year's Day. Anything earlier or later is simply overkill and should be punishable by enduring an obscene snow sculpture in the front yard or a yellow snow bank near the driveway.

7. The Decorative Christmas Tree Sweater

See that middle-aged woman wearing the blinking, illuminated sweater with the matching candy cane socks? Want to annoy her as much as her outfit has annoyed you? Don't say a word to her about the attire. Don't even fake a compliment. To this grandma wannabe, acknowledgment equals encouragement.

8. Real Trees Versus Fake

Let's see . . . One requires hard labor in the bitter cold, and it ultimately poses a very real fire hazard. Your other choice requires about ten minutes to set up, and it fits nicely under the basement stairs for the other eleven months of the year. 'Nuff said.

9. Tipping

I'm sure some etiquette guides suggest that during the holidays it's considered good form to tip service providers like hairdressers, postal carriers, dog groomers, day care providers, newspaper carriers, parking attendants, and so on. Since none of these are my own profession, I don't really care what you do. But here's a tip: Give Christmas presents to your children's teachers shortly before grades are given out. This way you can tell friends at holiday parties that your children are at the top of their classes and have the recent evidence to prove it.

10. The Santa Cap

It's just not funny. Never was, never will be. And it certainly doesn't give you a proper excuse to offer your lap as a seat to guests.

11. Music

Best Christmas song ever? Band Aid's 1984 hit "Do They Know It's Christmas?" Worst Christmas song ever? A tie between "Grandma Got Run Over By a Reindeer" and José Feliciano's "Feliz Navidad" (not to be confused with Nachos Navidad, a much more satisfying staple of the season). Take note, and fill your iPod party mix accordingly, please.

12. Drinking Before Midnight Mass

Look at it this way, and then never do it again. The savior of the world was born, and you're going to show up trashed at His birthday party? Happy Birthday, Jesus! Forgive this guy. But please note, he's not with me. I'm the one two pews behind him fluctuating between disgust and repressed fascination watching him grope his fiancée during the moment of shared peace.

— — —

So what's your reward for surviving a blitz of Christmas parties? Enduring the most boring day of the year: December 25. Nothing's on television, stores are closed, and you've become a virtual prisoner trapped inside your own home. Maybe that's for the best because you'd better rest up. The Night of all Nights is fast approaching.

NEW YEAR'S EVE

Remember when this was the Night of the Year? You spent months planning where you'd be at midnight, who you'd be with, what you'd wear, and what you'd be drinking. You wouldn't be caught dead staying home during this social event of the season.

Now, as adulthood sets in, you can't be caught awake past 11 P.M. One of the last times I was upright to ring in the new year, I entertained myself by standing in the doorway in my pajamas and shouting at teenagers who were shooting off fireworks, telling them, "Yeah baby! Light up the sky! Thanks for the show!" Wild stuff, I know.

A lot of my friends tell me they stay in on New Year's Eve just to avoid the amateur night antics of young drunks in the restaurants, in the bars, and worse, on the roads. The reason Kelly and I often stay home is usually a result of my unsuccessful efforts in trying to snag a restaurant reservation a week before the big night. To my shock and dismay, this usually causes a spat in my house. *I called about 168 hours in advance! What's half-assed about that?* Well, according to Kelly and her friends, my approach is in fact considered quite half-assed. So learn from my mistakes, and make plans much earlier than you know is really necessary.

If your spouse is like mine, she will consider your Dinner for Two socially insufficient. That means after dessert you're running head first into a party largely comprised of professional adults, with only a few accidental adults to keep you company. Well . . . relax. I've been there before, and I'll bet this looks familiar to you too:

ASSIMILATED ADULT	ACCIDENTAL ADULT
Knows the words to several verses of "Auld Lang Syne."	Wonders how anyone could remember words to a song they hear only once a year and sing only while they're drunk.

ADVICE This night is your annual chance for harmless fun. I'm talking about abruptly kissing someone who isn't your spouse. Maybe even a few people. So spend time remembering the names of the people you want to peck rather than memorizing ancient Scottish song lyrics. At midnight it won't feel like you're kissing strangers, which would be impolite, not to mention disrespectful to your spouse.

ASSIMILATED ADULT	ACCIDENTAL ADULT
Confides that after years of breaking New Year's resolutions, this year her resolution is to not make any more resolutions!	Instantly resolves to leave the party if he hears this unoriginal declaration again.

ADVICE Announcing your New Year's resolution is a great way to fool people into thinking you're a profoundly reflective and motivated adult—unless you're just resolving to take fewer naps like I did one year. Consider making a bolder commitment, and one that requires no evidence or corroboration. Like offering up a daily prayer for your enemies. Or visualizing world peace. Who's to say?

ASSIMILATED ADULT	ACCIDENTAL ADULT
Corrects you when you refer to your glass of sparkling wine as champagne, saying, "It's not champagne unless it comes from the region of France called Champagne."	Wishes his glass were full of beer from the region of Milwaukee instead, and his drinking partner didn't have a stick up his ass.

ADVICE Swallow your sparkling wine along with your pride and move to the buffet table. Feigning interest in French carbonated alcohol only fuels the ego of a self-important wine connoisseur, and it requires way more energy than you have at midnight.

On the ride home, congratulate yourself for surviving the most over-rated evening of the year. Who stays up this late anymore, anyway?

SUPER BOWL

This party annoys me more than any other gathering all year long. Here's why: On any given Sunday from September through January, I'll watch at least three to four hours of football, depending on a few variables:

- If the Green Bay Packers game is televised in my Minnesota television market.
- If the Sunday Night Football game features teams that don't suck.
- If Kelly has determined that I've met my familial obligations that weekend. This usually involves helping kids with homework, raking leaves, fixing the laptop, paying the bills, packing Monday's lunches, or any other petty task inconsequential to my own personal and selfish enjoyment.

I'm far from a diehard sports fan, and I'd say devoting this amount of time to watching football is hardly excessive. But I've always been a sucker for conflict, competition, a good story, and televised violence with instant replay. In that way, the NFL usually delivers.

So after five months of keeping up with my favorite team and the breakdowns from other teams around the league, the last thing I want to do during the definitive game of the season is to share the experience over the din of men's shouting, women's shrieking, and children's complaining—all while standing in a corner for four hours holding a soggy plate of bean dip and chips. If you find yourself in this unenviable position, cue your smart-ass inner monologue survival skills to muddle through these inevitably unavoidable situations.

Commercial Lover

Woman: "I guess I'm a bit unusual. I watch the Super Bowl just for the commercials!"

Outward response: "That's really unique!"

Inner monologue: *Yes, you and about every one of the other 150 million women in America!*

She's obviously out of her element here, which is a feeling any accidental adult can routinely relate to in most circumstances. So just punt. Ask her which commercial she liked best, and when she mentions the lame one that featured dancing animals, politely agree and be grateful she didn't mention the nervous giggling she heard from the men at the keg during the erectile dysfunction ad. At least she's not acting like some of the other women who suddenly became football's biggest fans just today.

The Clever Chef

Host: "Won't this be fun? We planned our menu around the Super Bowl city! Hope you like New Orleans–style Cajun cuisine!"

Outward response: "I always love to try new food!"

Inner monologue: *Where the hell are my weiner winks?*

NOTE TO
PROFESSIONAL ADULTS

Don't get cute here. I have to pretend to enjoy your delightful goat cheese risotto and your battered eggplant appetizers at every other party you throw throughout the year. Today's the day I get to sample chili, wings, pizza, and nachos all on one big-ass sloppy plate.

The Ex-Jock Know-It-All

It's no surprise that sports-themed parties bring out the wannabe coaches and the used-to-be players. Makes you want to say, "I get it,

I get it. You played a little ball back in the day before you blew out your knee during the big game. Somehow, you've now become more qualified to call plays than that dumb-ass millionaire NFL coach." Recognize this?

Ex-jock know-it-all: "That quarterback is an idiot! Why is he throwing off his back foot into double coverage?"

Outward response: "I was about to say the same thing!"

Inner monologue: *I like it when the quarterback throws the ball really far.*

Guess what? I don't want to hear you scream at the fifty-inch plasma calling for a split-back formation or the play-action pass. What will really impress me is if you chop block that meathead at the other end of the room who deserves a holding penalty for cornering victims and bragging about how his fantasy football team kicked ass this year.

– – –

Listening to your inner monologue might keep you company for only a few hours, but it should make one thing clear: This party doesn't deserve an instant replay next year.

DINNER PARTIES

They say that sharing a meal with family or friends is one of the most important social bonding experiences available to humans because it nourishes both body and soul. I'm never quite sure who "they" are exactly, but I'd sure like to ask "them" why so many people have to ruin a good thing by overdoing it. Of course I'm talking about the dinner party. The pinnacle of fine entertainment. The bastion of home-based hospitality. The dreaded fly in my proverbial soup.

I'm all for a little elegance and culture with my meals every now and again. But when it comes to the dinner party, accidental adults tend to feel thrown off their game, largely because the real adults hold the home field advantage—and many of them keep score.

- ✓ Did you forget to remove the napkin from the glass at the proper moment?
- ✓ Did you salt and pepper your food before tasting it?
- ✓ Did you cut up your entire steak in one shot, instead of slicing a piece and eating as you go?
- ✓ Did you place a dirty utensil directly on the table instead of on the plate?
- ✓ Did you excuse yourself from the table during the meal? (*Too many cocktails consumed while waiting for the meal to be frickin' served already!*)

The first dinner party Kelly and I threw as a married couple was in our cramped two-bedroom apartment. Not to be deterred by our limited space, we decided to invite eight coworkers of mine for a fun little get-together. We brought out our new china, gold-plated flatware, and our crystal stemware, freshly unpacked from our stack of mostly useless (but suddenly appreciated) wedding gifts. We bought liquor and wine that we had never purchased before, just so the adults could feel at home when getting their drink on. And all in all, we entertained our guests with considerable class—for a couple of twentysomethings.

Or so we thought. Later at work, I learned that despite our best efforts at sophisticated entertaining, we needed a little help. Our biggest gaffe? We unknowingly broke the "one starch at a meal" rule by serving pasta *and* potatoes. Who knew?

I'll tell you who knew. The real adults we invited. Fortunately for us, these friendly fortysomethings politely taught us kids a few tricks of the trade for successful dinner partying. Buoyed by their advice, and wisened from my own mistakes along the way, I can repay my ancient colleagues by paying it forward to you with some simple dos and don'ts.

When breaking bread with friends, don't break these rules:

The Table Setting

If your hosts' fine china is so fine that you're scared shitless to look at it, let alone eat off of those platinum-trimmed plates, just relax. You probably won't be asked (or allowed) to clear the table at the end of the evening. Take a seat, and take these cues:

DO . . .	DON'T . . .
Openly admire the elegant tableware. But be sure to clearly enunciate when you tell the hostess her china looks great tonight.	Announce you'd like to sell your wife's tableware on eBay, since she only uses it once a decade.
Toast the host with gratitude for a classy evening.	Smack your crystal champagne flute with your neighbor's and offer a hearty "bottom's up."
Compliment the hostess on the centerpiece she chose, especially if its height effectively blocks your sightline across the table from any undesirable guest you were hoping to avoid.	Attempt to eat the centerpiece's plastic fruit or ask "so who gets this thing after tonight?"

The Meal

Okay, you've survived seven hours of painful predinner conversation numbed only by the limited number of cocktails your spouse allowed you to enjoy (despite your pronouncement in the car ride to the party that tonight you're getting really messed up). Dinner is about to be served. It's go time.

DO . . .	DON'T . . .
Eat everything you're offered, no matter how unusual it seems.	Ask the hostess to warm up your soup that's gone cold. It's gazpacho, Señor Suave.
Switch to drinking the alcohol being served at the table.	Bring your half-empty can of Coors Light to the table, along with an unopened backup.
Swallow the fat.	Gag (if you can help it).

The Conversation

You don't need a reminder that religion and politics are taboo topics. But isn't it trite to talk about work or the weather? So what do you share in conversations with complete strangers that won't expose you for the accidental adult that you are? Let's talk . . .

DO . . .	DON'T . . .
Politely agree with everything that's said or play devil's advocate as necessary in order to keep the conversation flowing in a way that keeps others talking, so you can continue eating.	Overshare. That means no tales about your medical history, your pending court date (no matter how trumped up the charges are), or your hygiene habits, unless you enjoy awkward silences. . . .

DO . . .	DON'T . . .
Nod often and gaze wistfully into space to demonstrate thoughtful contemplation when participating in complex conversations with intelligent people.	Become too eager to interrupt those conversations with agreements of "I know" or "Exactly." It's possible your conversation partner could stop talking and ask you to share what it is you know, exactly.
Make safe observational comments about other guests that demonstrate your awareness of their positive characteristics, like, "You're clever! Are you in advertising?" or "You're really well informed! What are you reading these days?"	Say, "You're not drinking! Are you the designated driver?" or "You're really starting to show now! When is the baby due?" Guess what? The alcoholic and the woman who gained weight after her hysterectomy won't be impressed by your keen observations.

As the evening winds down and the hostess asks if you're interested in a nightcap, try not to snicker. She's not inviting you upstairs like they do in the movies, and she's likely making the same offer to everyone present. Politely accept her offer as a reward for surviving your high-stakes evening. And remember, nightcap is singular, not plural.

SUMMER PATIO PARTY: YOUR TIME TO SHINE

There's something of an unspoken rule in many households that the inside is the wife's domain while the outside is the man's fiefdom. In our house, any creative ideas I'd like to suggest for furniture purchases, window coverings, paint color selection, or any other interior decorating exercises are largely considered unwelcome. Conversely, if Kelly wants to chime in on landscaping or lawn maintenance issues, she'll likely be met with a blank stare.

This same code of conduct should apply to entertaining. The minute a party moves outdoors, the responsibility for ensuring an enjoyable evening shifts from hostess to host, especially when the host is an accidental adult. Why? The hot summer night backyard party may be the only social event of the year where accidental adult protocol virtually trumps standard adult-cult etiquette every time. So this is your moment to shine. It's summertime, and the livin' should be easy. That means you get to clutch a plastic cup of keg-tapped beer, stretch out in a lawn chair, and gnaw a few spareribs to the bone. And because the party's outside, your instinctual conduct actually conforms in this case to society's behavioral expectations for adults (in this venue).

Achieving this entertainment utopia is not without its challenges, however. In the wrong adult hands, your patio party can quickly turn from nirvana into an unnecessarily refined and overly contrived celebration. The trick is keeping the professional adults at bay. That means taking over the planning and execution of the event yourself. As you do, consider the following checklist of Patio Party Pointers to throw a summer bash, accidental adult style.

PATIO PARTY POINTERS

The Barbecue Grill

First off, leave charcoal grilling to those old-school adults who know how to coax the coals into submission. For the impatient accidental adult, propane power is the only way to go.

Next, make certain that nothing other than meat and the occasional vegetable ever touches your grill. Contrary to what your refined friends may think, the grill is no place to lightly sear some exotic fruit or prepare any other cutsey hors d'oeuvres for your guests. These pointlessly pretentious extravagances take up valuable grill space that could more appropriately accommodate another beef kabob or two.

The Refreshments

The party doesn't start until you tap the keg, so you better brush up on your tapping skills:

Step 1: Remove the plastic beer label cap and place it face up on the top of the keg. This way, everyone knows you broke the bank and bought the good stuff (this time). Note to college-aged or piss-poor accidental adults: do not display the Pabst Blue Ribbon cap. Dispose of it immediately and tell your buddies it's Heineken.

Step 2: Position the tap over the seal, push down, twist clockwise, and lock it into place.

Step 3: Take a moment to towel dry your face, arms, and chest after becoming soaked by the pressurized beer that shoots from the seal each time you unsuccessfully attempt to perform Step 2.

Step 4: Pump the tap, pour a beer, and proudly present that first foamy glass to the buddy who laughed the loudest when you sprayed beer up your nose.

If a tapped keg signals the start of the party, then remember that a fried keg means the party's over. After inviting eighty friends to a backyard party and ordering only one half-barrel, I learned this lesson far too late in life. When the keg ran dry at 9:30 P.M., I didn't have time to make another liquor store run. Thankfully, some responsible adult neighbors came to my rescue and emptied their refrigerators of all things alcohol to fuel our party past 11 P.M. Despite accusations to the contrary, this was not a shrewd strategic move to pull the plug on our party and get a good night's sleep. Call it yet another humiliating adventure on my reluctant journey.

Yard Games

Why, oh why must every party include a planned, organized activity? Don't force the fun (unless it's beer pong). Lawn darts and alcohol are never a good combination anyway. Instead, consider the best one-two punch of backyard entertainment ever . . .

The Backyard Band

A party with an iPod and speakers is just a party. But a party with a decent, fun, and funny band is a blast. The key to a great soundtrack is finding a group that plays your kind of music (for me it's alternative rock or anything from the '80s) and not your parents' oldie moldie favorites. This means Elvis, the Beatles, the Beach Boys, and the Temptations are not on your guest list. Also not invited? Steve Miller, Lynyrd Skynyrd, Fleetwood Mac, or any other band known as classic rock. Remember, if you're paying for the music, you get to call the shots. I first flexed this musical muscle when I hired my wedding band with the stipulation that if they played Bob Seger's "Old Time Rock and Roll" I wouldn't pay them a dime. Thanks to my meddling, I'm happy to say there were no guests at my wedding laying on the dance floor and kicking their legs in the air doing the *Risky Business* dance. Quite the triumph, I'd say.

Fireworks

Following the backyard band's fourth and final encore, the perfect nightcap for any accidental adult's summertime get-together is, of course, an explosive pyrotechnic display. But much like building a bonfire, setting off fireworks is best left to the hyper-masculine über-male, not the easygoing, fire-challenged accidental adult. Every neighborhood has that guy who buys carloads of illegal fireworks and lives for the opportunity to blow off a case or two. (Hint: it's probably not you.) So befriend that firestarter, and enjoy the show from a safe distance.

DÉJÀ BREW

No matter if you were the host or the guest, you'll probably spend a good amount of time after any get-together second-guessing your party performance aloud with your spouse. For me, the afterglow usually goes something like this:

- "Do I really have to help your co-worker retile his bathroom next Saturday, or does he realize that's just something you say?"
- "Was that a 'Save me!' hand sign I saw that woman use to her husband when I was telling her about my marathon training regimen?"
- "Was it rude to vacuum before the guests left?" (OK, this one would best fit under Kelly's self-evaluation.)

I think most accidental adults perform these postparty appraisals as a means of improving their precarious position in the adults' world. But whatever the reason, a little self-reflection and self-improvement never hurt anyone. Be sure to leave a little time, however, for the unfortunate, yet inevitable, side effect that often accompanies a great party.

POST-PARTY DEPRESSION

After all the effort you've put into your event, it's only natural to feel a little depressed the day after throwing a killer party. Especially when you spent a month's worth of weekly staff meetings pretending to pay attention to your coworkers' "client-centric!" directives, while actually drawing up the guest list, planning the iPod party mix, and estimating the number of burger buns you'd need to buy. We call this melancholic low point *post-party depression*. It usually kicks in while you're performing the morning-after cleanup ritual—hosing off the driveway, mulching broken hotdogs and brats into the yard with your lawn mower, and searching all perimeters of your house for the empty beer bottles your buddies have hidden on their traditional "Screw You Scavenger Hunt." (Time-saving hint: Nine times out of ten, you'll find one inside the toilet tank. Fan out from there.)

As you break out the cold deli tray leftovers and reminisce over the night's most memorable moments, don't be too down. Instead, congratulate yourself for enduring yet another attempt at mass adult assimilation and surviving with your accidental adulthood firmly intact. We all may not aspire to the lofty entertainment heights of the Martha Stewarts or the Wolfgang Pucks of the world, but a little forced external class and a lot of natural internal sass can take you a long way. Maybe even past midnight sometime.

Party on!

us never planned o
is happening. But it di
ometime between gra
chool and our first mort
age, a strange phenom
non began replacing ou
outhful mojos with
ew-found maturity. An
e didn't see it coming
ur two-door coupe
orphed into sliding
or minivans. Bar-hop
ng turned into movi
ghts on the couch. No
e write letters to th

6. PARENTING

Do as I Say, *Definitely* Not as I Do

"AND WILL YOU, Colin and Kelly, accept children lovingly from God and bring them up according to the law of Christ in this church?"

This $64,000 question was posed to me and Kelly about a dozen years ago by "Smitty," my dad's best friend who was also his lifelong drinking buddy. Okay, so Smitty was now an ordained Catholic priest known by his parishioners as Father Smithes and this was my wedding day, but it still felt a bit strange. Decades earlier, Smitty and my dad did their share of carousing through scores of Milwaukee bars, and now here he was—one of God's holy disciples—about to bestow on me a sacrament that hinged on the answer to that camouflaged question, which sounded more like a thinly veiled command, direct from Rome.

"We will," was our reply.

So there it was. A simple answer to a life-altering question. And by declaring our kid commitment in front of God, our friends, our families, and a bunch of my new mother-in-law's friends whom I still don't

> "I won't lie to you. Fatherhood isn't easy like motherhood."
>
> —Homer Simpson

[99]

know, the message became very clear: "You promised, so don't screw this up. People are watching."

Fast forward to today, and I'm happy to say we've kept up our end of the bargain. After four early years of relative freedom, Kelly and I were finally blessed with a child—a red-haired, super-sensitive, super-sweet girl we named Shanley. In the years since, we've welcomed our easygoing, charming, red-haired son Finnegan and their dark-haired, unflappable baby sister Maeve, who belts out show tunes with the zest of a miniature Broadway diva. Yes, we're blessed with three healthy, entertaining, and beautiful children.

So I know what you're thinking. He's expressed gratitude and love for his children, right? Now that he's got that out of the way, here comes another one of those whiny missives where a self-pitying dad bemoans the agonies of fatherhood. About how tough it can be to smile at bedtime after enduring a dinner interrupted *twice* by "Daddy, will you wipe me?" shouted from the bathroom followed by a bathtime punctuated with tortured screams of "You're getting shampoo in my eyes, Daddy!" Or maybe you're expecting to hear how exhausting it is to work in an office all day and then be expected to give piggyback rides and play hide-and-go-seek at night. Or about how sobering it is when you realize that now you're supposed to be a moral compass and shining example for three impressionable gifts from God when your list of personal heroes includes Tommy Lee and Chris Farley.

Well . . . you'd be right. But hey, indulge me. I'll give you a few tips to help you pose like a professional, responsible parent without ever becoming someone whose happiness revolves around the outcome of a Little Squirt's T-ball game. If you're successful, you might even trick your kids into thinking you know what you're doing.

Oh, and I'll try to take it easy on the whining.

CHAMPIONS OF INCONSISTENCY

If you're like me, then I'll bet we share a trait that's fairly common to the accidental adult parent: inconsistency. Your motto may as well be "Do as I say, not as I do" because if your kids paid really close attention to you—or worse, if they could get inside your brain for a day—here's what they'd discover:

DO AS I SAY . . .	NOT AS I DO . . .
It seems like every hour of the day you tell your children to put away their toys, straighten up their bedrooms, and never leave a mess for others to clean.	Yet a dozen times every day you will walk past a hammer that you left on top of the clothes dryer until your wife inconveniently asks you to strain yourself and put it back in that Tupperware basket you call a tool box that's in the shelf a distant two feet above the dryer.
The first time your toddler son urinated on a tree in the front yard in broad daylight, you scooped him up and brought him inside to finish his business, then you explained about privacy, boundaries, and bathroom etiquette.	The second time he peed on your lawn, you realized he was modeling *your* behavior—recalling that incident when you were digging up monster weeds from the forest in your backyard and your wife refused you entry to the house until you cleaned yourself up a bit. (So whose fault is it?)
When you inquire about the status of your children's homework, they turn up the volume of the television to tune you out, earning themselves a direct trip to their room for a grounding.	When your wife inquires about the status of the junk in the garage, you cram your fingers in your ears and perform the "na-na-na-na-na-I-can't-hear-you" song, earning yourself a direct trip to the garage.

DO AS I SAY . . .

When your kids ask if they can watch a movie at a friend's house, you call the friend's parents and ask them what the movie is rated to ensure they're not bombarded with sexuality, adult language, or violence.

You teach your kids the importance of promptness and preparation, like being dressed and ready for the school bus each morning and taking responsibility for their daily belongings.

When your son joins a devious neighborhood game of playing catch with pumpkins in your driveway, you put a stop to the action before you have broken shells, sticky seeds, and a stringy orange splatter strewn across your property.

Like all responsible parents, you withhold dessert until your children eat the vegetables or fruit on their dinner plates.

NOT AS I DO . . .

Yet when your buddy forced you and the guys to see the new James Bond film at your most recent Guys' Movie Night, you vehemently objected to the pick because the movie reviewer said the most brutal violence occurs offscreen, and it doesn't feature nudity. (Not even partial!)

But when you hit the snooze alarm one too many times, and you're now stumbling through the kitchen at 9:15 in the morning rushing toward your 9:30 A.M. meeting, you instinctually start shouting, "Honey, where the hell did you put my black dress shoes and my winter gloves? Now I'm going to be late!"

Yet you secretly wish your wife would relent already and let you bring the boy up onto your roof to show him how you launched a few rotten jack-o'-lanterns onto your back patio a few years ago, just so you could marvel in the beautiful and harmless mess.

Like all accidental adults, you can't possibly find room on your own plate for anything green because you've loaded it up with nacho chips.

It's not that you're a hypocrite . . . it's just that . . . well, yeah, you're a hypocrite. And what's worse is you should have seen this coming, but you didn't. And neither did I.

A PARENTAL POSEUR

Like most accidental adults, I was caught completely off-guard when I became a father, which is rather remarkable considering I willingly participated in several rounds of outcome-based procreation. I shouldn't complain; I knew the end result. But I had no idea that fatherhood meant fast-tracking my reluctant journey to adulthood— a foreign land where feeling out of place has become a near daily experience for me. A place where the neighborhood kids would call me "Mr. Sokolowski," and I'm supposed to keep a straight face. A place where I would be expected to know the answers to questions like "Why can I see the moon in the morning?" and "Where does our pee end up after we flush the toilet?" A place where I'm required to provide a more reasoned response to the question "Can I have some of that cake for breakfast, Daddy?" than simply offering a knee-jerked "Hell no! Daddy's hungry too you know."

I'm sure full-blooded adults can breeze through parental litmus tests like those. For them, parenthood feels natural. But not for me. After nearly a decade of practice, I still feel like a parental poseur . . . an arbitrary authority figure . . . a freakin' fraud. In fact, there's no other role I play in which I feel so out of my element. Hey, I can fake my way through a NASCAR conversation with my brother-in-law. I'm even quite convincing when discussing a few of the more popular crabgrass treatment options with neighbors (having inadvertently learned a lesson or two following a few late-summer invasions). But unless I'm more careful, my kids are going to call me out and expose me for the reluctant grownup I really am—much sooner than I'd like. Why?

I'm the guy who repeatedly buys peanut-laced treats when it's our turn to bring the school snack to share. "Didn't you know that's not allowed, Daddy?" You'd think I would.

I'm the guy who picks up his daughter from a birthday party and asks the only other adult male in the house which little girl he's picking up. "He lives here, Daddy. His daughter is the birthday girl." Right. Should've just kept my mouth shut.

I'm the guy who will occasionally run through a grocery store, sprinting down the aisles, sometimes jumping onto the shopping cart's lower-shelf to temporarily glide for a while, even if I'm wearing a sport coat, tie, and dress shoes. "Daddies don't run inside stores! You look like a kid!" Just keep up with me. Your mother is waiting in our God-forsaken minivan, and your brother is driving her nuts.

I wish I could say these events make my wife feel my pain, but they don't—and she doesn't. Motherhood comes easier to Kelly than fatherhood fits for a guy like me. Sure, she gets overwhelmed and frustrated by the kids sometimes. She even has to endure the occasional judgments from sanctimommies—women who are much, much better mothers than Kelly and who sometimes wonder aloud, "Why can't her kids swim yet?" or "Why is she drinking a glass of wine at her daughter's birthday party?" (God no!)

But she never looks like an actor playing an unfamiliar role. Nope. Kelly was a natural mom even before she had kids. She was the one at the party who'd brush past the buffet table and make a beeline for the hostess's baby, grabbing the tiny bundle and planting the wobbly kid on her hip for the rest of the night. My interest in the infant would wane after about half a beer, and then it was back to my corner of the room where I could hear the music better.

In performing the role of a lifetime, I'm amazed at how often I find myself ad-libbing through scene after scene while Kelly seems to have all the right parenting lines memorized. Like a lot of accidental adult parents who feel less prepared than their spouse, I can't help but wonder, "How come she didn't give me a proper audition?" or "What do I do if I get stage fright?" or on some of the few good days, "Can I get an award for this performance?"

YOU CAN'T AFFORD TO SCREW THIS UP

By necessity, I've evolved a bit since those earlier days, and I even occasionally feel proud of the progress I've made. I've developed a new perspective on life, all because of my kids. How can any parent not? Whether you're an intentional adult or an accidental adult, parenthood forever changes you. You notice things differently now, especially if you're a guy. We pay more attention to the baby diaper changing stations in men's rooms than the condom dispensing machines. When you're watching the game on TV with your son, you change the channel in a flash when a beer commercial comes on featuring female mud wrestlers, but not before hitting the TiVo "record" button in case you can't sleep later tonight. We're quick to scowl when we hear foul language spewed at state fairs or sports events, whereas not too long ago we were the ones dropping the F-bomb a little too loudly in mixed company.

And no matter how uncomfortable or unnatural you feel in the role of a parent, you realize this is the one job in life you really can't afford to screw up. You'll do whatever it takes so your children can find success and leave their unique marks upon the world. Unfortunately for some of us dads, that often means trying to create instant replays of our own childhoods, or at least the revisionist histories we've created where we always win the big game, get the girl, and snag the full-ride college scholarship.

But if you're an accidental adult like me, you never won the big game, and you didn't lose much sleep over it, either. Ergo, your child-rearing philosophy is probably a bit different. Sure you want to act your age when you have to and care about the things adults seem to care about, but you also don't want to lose your cool quotient and start wearing dark socks with Bermuda shorts. You don't want to transform from a caring provider to a consumed and meddling helicopter parent, hovering overhead, rarely out of your children's reach, and taking your role a little too seriously. Not the accidental adult.

Our approach is a bit more laissez faire and a lot more liberating. It's not that we don't care about our kids' math curriculum at school. We just won't organize a committee to fire the principal if classroom test scores dropped by a half of a percentage point last semester. It's not that we don't care that our kids' Youth Dribblers basketball team didn't run the pick and roll properly last weekend. We just won't ask the volunteer coach to supplement his drills by distributing diagram handouts because you think the children are cognitive thinkers who respond better to visually learning, not kinesthetic lessons. It's not that we don't care if the kids decide they don't want to sing in the children's Christmas choir that rehearses across town every Saturday morning for two months. Well, yeah, we don't really care about that one.

So how can you ignore a few norms yet raise normal kids? Allow me to submit what I'd like to call . . .

THE MARGINALLY MATURE PARENT'S PRIMER FOR RAISING KIDS WITHOUT SELLING OUT

Child development studies show that children demonstrate strong indicators of their future character and personality by the age of three. That's not much time to influence them to become the coolest person possible—modeled after you!

For Parents of Girls

☑ Allow them to pick any instrument they want to play. (Except for the flute. Too conventional, predictable.)

☑ So they want to join Girl Scouts? Great! So long as they agree they won't sell cookies. It's part of the sacred Scout agreement, they say? Then ask them how much profit they need to clear, and come up with the cash yourself. There are better places to learn life lessons about giving guilt and receiving rejection than on your neighbors' doorsteps.

☑ Discourage them from giving you a button with a photo of them in their leotard from dance class or gymnastics. Because if they do, and you don't wear it, then you're a jerk. If you do wear it, then you may as well buy a Members Only jacket to pin it on and zip it up tightly over your short-sleeve button-down dress shirt and knit tie, or maybe even consider taking up mall walking. Wearing buttons like these is exactly what grandparents are for. They already have an outfit that complements these buttons perfectly.

☑ Make them a deal. You know those Saturday swim team fundraisers where the sixteen-year-olds stand on the street corner waving carwash signs to passing motorists? If your girls promise they won't ever join those bouncing, shrieking, bikini-clad girls, you swear you'll always keep your vision focused straight ahead and your foot off the brake as you cruise through the intersection.

For Parents of Boys

- ☑ Help them maintain a nice little circle of grubby, naughty, and funny friends, but also show them how to play politely with the girls. Don't let them become that typical little creep who throws mud on the girls or calls them names. They have no idea how well their coed chivalry at six years old will pay off when they get older. (Your sons may even thank you later.)

- ☑ Chances are, if you never buy them a pair of hockey skates, they won't cultivate that interest. Mission accomplished! You'll save thousands of dollars, gain countless hours of Saturday morning slumber, and maintain a reasonable core body temperature. If that sounds a bit harsh, then let them choose any fair-weather (60°F or warmer) sport or activity, and you'll promise to be there.

- ☑ Remind them that it's cool to kiss their dad, even in public, no matter how old they are. If Eddie Van Halen can kiss his sixteen-year-old son on stage in front of 20,000 roaring and drunk middle-aged fans, then your son can let you plant one on his cheek when you pick him up from school.

- ☑ At what age is it appropriate for your son to watch *Star Wars*, *Jaws*, or any other cool monster, science-fiction, or violent war movie? Whenever he can convincingly explain to Mommy that Daddy didn't show it to him first. He saw it at a friend's house. Dads, back him up in this harmless yarn. But as a tradeoff for your complicity, you're on midnight bedside duty when his recurring nightmares begin.

For Parents of All Children

- ☑ Teach them to never be intimidated by adults. Trust me. They're not all as smart and self-assured as you'd think.

- ☑ Encourage them to assemble a few good smart-ass retorts ready for any occasion that makes them feel uncomfortable. Then tell them to keep those comments to themselves. They can share them with you when they're old enough to hear all of your inner monologue rants.

- ☑ Give them a balanced exposure to the three As: academics, arts, and athletics. Last time I checked, "well balanced" describes the kids who do more than play four seasons of sports or spend all day buried in books and schoolwork.

- ☑ Most importantly, show them how to always, always, always clap on two and four.

A successful childhood shouldn't necessarily hinge on your kids fulfilling every wish on that list. It would just make your life easier. And for me, that's a primary goal these days. After consecutive mornings of kids coughing across my breakfast and brokering peace accords because someone sneaked an extra Flintstones vitamin . . . well, frankly I could use a little help.

JUST ANOTHER FRAZZLED FATHER?

You might say I should take considerable comfort in knowing that I'm not alone in facing the challenges of fatherhood. But that doesn't help. To be honest, I'd rather think that I really am an island among dads. That way, I'd be an especially sympathetic and praiseworthy dad. So whenever those bubble-bursters tell me I'm just like all the other frazzled fathers out there, I politely smile and force myself to

agree with them. Inside, I'm still not sure what a full-blooded adult
dad is supposed to be—I just know that I'm not it. And neither are
many accidental adults. Especially the kind of fathers that most retailers think we should be—judging by those "Gifts for Dads" displays
that pop up in stores around Father's Day.

Music for Dads: Are we really supposed to buy CD box sets of James
Taylor, Jimmy Buffet, and The Doobie Brothers, just because we
procreated? Sure, I'll admit it. I've seen Neil Diamond in concert a few times. I was even singing "Bah-bah-bum" to "Sweet
Caroline" long before it was cool. But I'm prouder to say I've seen
Mötley Crüe, Ratt, and Prince several times, and at an age when
more responsible fathers were spending their hard-earned money
on family vacations and not on concert tickets.

Tools for Dads: When was the last time you got excited over a socket
wrench set or a wet/dry vacuum? Same here. So why do retailers
think these are the perfect gifts for fathers? Don't they know that
gifting a tool sends the wrong message to us accidental adults?
"Hey Daddy, you deserve a special treat that makes it easier for
you to perform manual labor in every spare moment you have!"

Clothes for Dads: By now, my family knows better than to give me
a snazzy tie or a smart pair of trousers, and I hope your family
does too. Yet too many clothing stores still think that most fathers
simply love a good cardigan or a pair of toasty wool slippers.
Like these stores, we accidental adults also are prone to delusional
thinking from time to time. We may not be fashion-forward
fathers, but most mornings, the guy we see in our dressing mir-
rors is more of a Banana Republic dad than a JCPenney dad.

Since I'll probably never morph into another Ward Cleaver watching the *Evening News* clenching my pipe every night, maybe the best I can hope for is to keep my accidental adult identity hidden from my kids—at least as long as possible. Someday I'll make a mangled model rocket with my son and pray he doesn't notice. Then later in school we'll build some shitty-ass LEGO robot that fails the morning of the science fair. And I'll certainly attempt to build a proper paper airplane for my kids, and then blame their throwing skills when it doesn't fly correctly. As long as my three children know I tried to help them, with love in my heart and obscenities held securely beneath my breath, that's all that matters. All those years ago, I promised God, Smitty, and Kelly that I'd bring kids into the world, and I'm happy I did. In spite of their maturity-challenged father, my cherished children will survive, and they will thrive. And yes, they will grow up.

Accidentally, I hope.

f us never planned
his happening. But it di
ometime between gra
chool and our first mort
age, a strange phenom
non began replacing ou
outhful mojos with
ew-found maturity. An
e didn't see it comin
ur two-door coupe
orphed into sliding
oor minivans. Bar-hop
ing turned into mov
ights on the couch. No
e write letters to t

7. TRANSPORTATION

SUVs and Minivans—It's How We Roll

MY JOURNEY FROM CHILDHOOD to accidental adulthood took place atop a black and purple 1986 Honda Spree scooter. And I couldn't be more proud.

I give full credit to those funky scooter commercials from the '80s. They played about every fifteen minutes on MTV, and I was there soaking it all in from the vantage of my corduroy beanbag chair slumped about two feet away from my parents' Zenith television set, changing channels with my toes in the harsh, pre–remote control era. There was the megalomaniac Chicago Bears quarterback Jim McMahon endorsing "outrageousness!" and "waking people up" with a scooter. Another spot featured the new wave band Devo (as if they weren't in MTV's rotation enough) encouraging viewers to "Choose a scooter that best expresses your individuality" and to "Always wear your helmet."

But my favorite ad was the one with the robotic and chiseled pop culture icon Grace Jones and pretty

"Ed, this is not the car I ordered. I distinctly ordered the Antarctic Blue Super Sports Wagon with the CB and the optional rally fun pack."

—Clark Griswold, *National Lampoon's Vacation*

boy British singer Adam Ant, whose playful exchange went something like this:

Grace Jones: *"It's easy! It's quick! It's fun! It's sexy!"*
Adam Ant: *"I'll take it!"*
Grace Jones: *"I'll take you!"* (Biting his ear.)
Announcer: *"Honda scooters. They're everything but ordinary."*

At sixteen years old, that's all I needed to hear.

"That's me!" I thought. "*I am everything but ordinary. In fact, I'm extraordinary! Where do I get one?*"

Looking back, I must have fit their target market perfectly: cash-strapped, media-manipulated, teenage male in need of transportation and hoping to boost his social status among high school females. So I emptied my savings of $450 and became one of the first in central Wisconsin to take a walk on the wild side astride a Honda Spree.

By that summer, though, my town's streets were besieged by high school scooter gangs—packs of punks wildly weaving and speeding through traffic on their black and red scooters. But I wasn't among them. Nope. When I kick-started my Purple Rain (yeah, I lamely named my black and purple scooter in honor of Prince), I left the claustrophobic confines of Marshfield (pop. 18,290) and imagined myself entering Lou Reed's New York City urban playground. When I was two blocks out of sight from my parents' house, I'd take off my mom-required (and Devo-endorsed) helmet, throw it into the make-shift basket on the back rack (a purple milk crate I strapped down with a series of bungee cords), and let my mullet blow free in the wind. And instead of joining a scooter gang, I chose to ride solo with only a Sony Walkman, earphones, and a few mix tapes of Duran Duran and Phil Collins for company.

But I was about to get a permanent copilot.

A few years after high school, I decided to haul my scooter to college 100 miles away in Minnesota, thinking it might transform me into the Big Man On Campus. You know . . . whipping past cute coeds on the way to Old Main . . . scooting around the campus quad . . . . Demented logic, really. In any event, my new ride did impress one especially sweet redhead who loved my scooter so much she offered to buy it. So in a moment of poverty-fueled weakness, I agreed to part with my beloved bike for the price of a semester's worth of textbooks.

Now, a few decades later, who knew such a deal would pay off?

Months after that babe bought Purple Rain, we started dating. Years later, we got engaged, and today she's my firecracker-of-a-wife and the beautiful mother of my kids. So now the joke goes, "Colin married Kelly to get his scooter back." Not exactly. But it was a tremendously appealing incentive. A 49cc dowry of sorts.

But like all dowries, this one came with strings attached— certain unspoken expectations thrust upon me by society and, more importantly, by my new wife. Now that I had essentially repo'ed my own scooter, there was an expectation that someday when I was older I would hang up the helmet, join the adult cult, and seek more responsible, family-friendly transportation. I knew this in the back of my twentysomething mind, but like most burgeoning accidental adults, I never really expected that day would arrive. Sadly for me, that harsh reality came screeching at me right around the corner. It's a good thing I know how to swerve.

SOCIAL MOBILITY

Taking Devo's advice (and who wouldn't?), I've decided that taking that helmet off the hook and kick-starting my scooter from time to time is a very cathartic way to express my individuality and to tap into that warm, fuzzy, retro place in my soul. That place where the biggest challenge in my life was figuring out how to advance to Level Five on Frogger and my heaviest responsibility was finding a coworker to take my shift at the bookstore so I could go to the DJ dance Friday night after the game. Considering how much more complicated life has become since those days, is it any wonder why I'd cherish a quick spin on my Purple Rain?

Some people believe that what you drive says a lot about you. If that's true, then every time I straddle my scooter and strap on my sensible DOT-approved helmet (I have to set an example for my kids now), I'm thumbing my nose at convention and shouting to the world: "That's right. I'm suffering from full-blown adult denial. So bite me!" I mean, think about it. What's more fitting for a reluctant grownup than tooling around town on a two-wheel throwback to the '80s—the best decade in history? In fact, I'd say my scooter serves as the perfect symbol for accidental adults like me. Some men work through their midlife crises by clinging to their souped-up Corvettes or buying testosterone-boosting motorcycles. That's what real men do. But not me. I'm searching for the road less traveled, because the main thoroughfare is coursing with ordinary adults, and that scares the hell out of me.

The only trouble with a father of three owning a scooter is that silly little nonsensical sticker attached to the steering column—the one that says "WARNING: OPERATOR ONLY. NO PASSENGERS." Which means my precious Purple Rain sits idle most months of the year in my garage parked next to a sensible sedan and a . . . (gulp) . . . minivan.

That sand-colored behemoth stands at the ready to haul my family around the balmy suburban Minneapolis/St. Paul area, and equally prepared to drive me to tears. Yes, it's the spacious solution for my family of five, and yes, it's easy to move around in. I can even make it from the front passenger seat to the rear bench in about three seconds flat with a plastic baggy in hand at the first sound of a car-sick child beginning to yack. But in my deepest, darkest, most shallow moments, I worry about the mixed message my van sends. If my scooter tells the world "I'm an accidental adult who's going down fighting," then my family van sends the exact opposite message. I mean, what better way to broadcast to the world "I've given up on my dreams" than with a minivan?

If cars are, as many believe, reflections of personalities, then what makes people choose the vehicle they drive? If you're like me, car sickness is what occurs when your monthly loan payment is due. That means it's your bank account's balance, not your indomitable persona, that will ultimately drive this decision. Unfortunately, this economically motivated choice inevitably produces a vehicle that tells the world you're scrimpin', not pimpin'. But let's suspend reality and pretend for one unrealistic moment that money doesn't matter. What vehicle would you drive? Careful. To the most small-minded among us, myself included, your decision will say a lot about you.

DARE TO COMPARE

SEDAN VERSUS SPORTS CAR

If you find yourself choosing between an everyday vanilla four-door sedan and a spicy two-door sports car, first take stock of your family situation.

Do you have children? If so, imagine which backseat interior space you'd like to hose down after an infant projectile vomits bananas and baby formula across the upholstery. The spacious back seat of a four-door or the cramped interior of a coupe? Imagine which car you'd like parked in the garage when your kids drag their bikes inside, scraping their handlebars against your vehicle and scratching the hell out of the side panels. A broken-in family sedan or a spiffy, smart sports car?

If you've concluded the sedan is the right choice, I'd say you're an intelligent, self-aware consumer who has sacrificed freedom for responsibility. Welcome to the club.

If, on the other hand, you are single or married with no children, first take a moment and feel my envy. Then go directly to your local car dealer and buy that flashy roadster that screams: Power! Status! Independence! Then take another moment to bathe in my red-hot resentment once again. Chances are, though, you'll soon be the stunned member of an expanding family (of your own doing), and I'll be smugly satisfied knowing you'll soon be facing your life's next biggest automotive buying dilemma . . .

MINIVAN VERSUS SUV

After our first child, Shanley, was born, Kelly and I debated what kind of vehicle she'd need in order to cart around a growing family. So I did some research, which usually annoys the hell out of her. This time was no different, especially because of what I discovered. When it comes to chauffering children around suburbia, there seemed to be two kinds of moms out there: Minivan Moms and what I like to call SUV PYTs (sports-utility-vehicle pretty-young-things).

As you might guess, the Minivan Mom chooses her vehicle because of its practicality and affordability. Deep down she may prefer something sportier, but it's not high on the priority list. And "sportier" doesn't really fit with her CD player loaded with the

Wiggle's "Yummy, Yummy" sing-along songs and her cup holders filled with crumpled-up juice boxes and sour-smelling sippy cups.

The SUV PYT, on the other hand, wouldn't be caught dead in a minivan (even though she might love the extra room of that magical stow-away third-row seat). To her, space and comfort are less important than bold styling and aggressive handling. She loves cranking Matchbox Twenty on her satellite radio connection, gabbing on her Bluetooth headset, and searching her dashboard GPS for the nearest Starbucks so she can sip another four-dollar grande latte. And as much as I hate to admit it, she usually looks damn good doing it.

So which of these vehicles is right for your family? That's your call entirely. But whatever you decide, please refrain from participating in that silent status battle between the Minivan Moms and the SUV PYTs. To me, those unapologetic minivan drivers are so much more attractive than the vocal minivan-haters who choose SUVs for status, not space. Likewise, a proud but silent SUV PYT is way hotter than the self-flagellating Minivan Mom who covets her neighbor's SUV while wallowing in her own self-pity. If you want to send your sympathy to someone who truly deserves it, I suggest you show some compassion for perhaps the most misguided vehicle owner of all . . .

PICKUP TRUCK VERSUS COMMON SENSE

I'm a firm believer that owning a pickup truck requires a particular pedigree. To begin, you must belong to a profession or participate in a hobby that requires you to haul large payloads on a regular basis—at least once a week (not twice a year). Next, it's reasonable to expect you to hunt, fish, camp, whitewater raft, or hike often. Your annual exotic mushroom hunt or urban bird watching excursions don't count. Finally, your temperament must be such that dings, scratches, and dents incurred while transporting materials in your cargo bed won't prompt ballistic outbursts of rage directed at people like me who foolishly believe it's quite appropriate to toss items at will into the back of your truck. (What, I have to be more careful? It's a trash-collecting, rusty *truck*, not a luxury vehicle! Maybe that tennis ball suspended from your garage ceiling to help you properly park should have told me you cared a little too much about your beloved vehicle.)

If for any reason you do not possess these aforementioned backgrounds, interests, or qualities, and if you and your spouse have started a growing family, then owning a pickup truck simply defies common sense, especially when so many other vehicles would suit your family's needs in a much more attractive manner. The trouble is, I know far too many parents who drive pickups without any legitimate towing or hauling justifications, and you probably do, too. When exactly did pickup trucks transform from sturdy, purposeful work vehicles to daily drive family cars anyway? And isn't it always a little bit jarring whenever you see a father unstrap his toddler from a child seat positioned on the bench seat of a pickup? Or when a middle-aged guy pulls into the parking space next to you in a compact pickup with a sticker on the rear window featuring that cartoon Calvin character pissing on the competitor's logo?

However this trend began, you can stop it. My advice? If you want your vehicle to tell the world you're a rugged rebel, forget the pickup truck and instead consider the following even less passenger-friendly rides . . .

MOTORCYCLE VERSUS SCOOTER

When my friend James turned forty, he treated himself to a 1980 Honda CB750 Custom motorcycle that he describes as "classic" and "vintage." I've offered other descriptions, like "clichéd" and "midlife crisis confirmation," but he dismisses these as the envious rants of a scooter owner who would ride a real man's road bike if only he could figure out how to shift gears without stripping the clutch. (He's not entirely wrong on that one.) However, James is guilty of two crimes commonly committed by many motorcycle enthusiasts and rarely perpetrated by scooter owners—offenses that are much more serious than simply succumbing to the anxiety accompanied by the onset of middle age.

His first crime is the Personification of a Motor Vehicle as evidenced by routinely referring to it as "she" and "her." Example: "She's a real sweet ride," and "I can't wait to take her out tonight." Of course, I'd be much harder on James for this offense if I hadn't named my scooter Purple Rain. But I was sixteen, not forty, and at no time was I ever confused as to its lack of humanity.

His second transgression is the Perpetuation of a Silent Social Hierarchy among Bikers. Apparently, as motorcyclists pass each other on the road, riders show respect for others' bikes by offering a slight wave or simply a brief nod. For James, it's a dropped left arm holding two fingers together, pointing down and away from his body. How kind! Unless you're a scooter driver or some punk on a neon-colored crotch rocket. If those subordinate bikers offer a gesture of acknowledgement or admiration to James and others of his ilk, no such signal is returned. Such is the sophomoric pecking order of motorcyclists.

Now which group would you want to join? If you're a real adult looking to make a trendy statement, then I suppose a motorcycle represents the most full-fledged commitment to rebellion and coolness that you can make. But if you're an accidental adult like me, half-assed declarations usually suffice.

USED VERSUS LEASED

If you're still suspending reality and pretending to believe that money doesn't matter (and thanks for continuing to play along!), then by all means zip down to your local car dealer and purchase a brand new vehicle that will depreciate some 30 percent within the first year after you peel out of the lot. Then forget about that lesson on fiscal responsibility you were preparing to deliver to your kids. You just lost your financial credibility (and your mind).

If, however, money isn't growing on your trees, then the real question is whether to buy a used car or lease one instead. Since my GRE math scores don't exactly position me as the best person to dispense economic advice, I'll leave this one up to you. But consider this. In my experience, the typical accidental adult is no stranger to accruing monthly fees for hanging onto overdue library materials or for exceeding monthly minutes on cell phone plans. I've even known a few who tell me about a barbaric and outrageous practice in which they often get nicked with overdraft fees from the bank simply for spending more money than they have in their account. (Bankers are way too serious!) If any of these absent-minded characteristics could apply to you, then heed my warning: Leased-vehicle agreements often contain mileage restrictions, body damage clauses, scheduled maintenance requirements, and penalties for early cancellations that could spell financial disaster if you're not paying attention. And since you know your kids are going to crap up the interior and scrape up the exterior, why sweat over every little stain and ding when the lease is up? Instead, enjoy the comforts of your mental fog and your general ambivalence and just buy a used car like the rest of us family guys. When you do, with all the pretension you can muster, refer to it lovingly thereafter as your "economically sensible preowned vehicle." If that arrogant term doesn't quite register with your childless, hipster friends (you know, the ones you typically envy), simply tell them that "preowned" also refers to the poor bastard who got "owned" by spending money on a brand new car only to sell it later at its depreciated value, dawg. (Are we still using "dawg?" No? Nevermind.)

ECONOMICS OVER IMAGE

In the end, choosing that minivan wasn't an easy decision for me. As much as I wanted Kelly to join that SUV PYT club (as did she), economics prevailed over image. And it was a bumpy road to travel.

On the day my dreams died, I entered the car dealership thinking, "If I lowball them, maybe they'll refuse the offer, but I'll look like a champ to Kelly just for trying. It's a win-win!" Turns out, it was a lose-lose. The dealer easily spotted an accidental adult attempting entry into the adults-only world of bargaining. Kelly kicked my leg under the table for trying to sabotage the deal. And before I knew it, I became the emasculated new owner of a seven-passenger dream killer.

So what's the antidote for an accidental adult who occasionally has to drive a minivan? For me, it's music. Almost immediately after sealing the deal on the "multipurpose-vehicle," my very next purchase was Van Halen's first album (on cassette of course) in order to alleviate the sinking feeling of hopeless maturity. Did it help? Not entirely. But I do find it somewhat liberating whenever I turn the key, pop in the tape, and lead my three small children in a rousing sing-along of "You Really Got Me" or "Ain't Talkin' 'Bout Love." The first time I auditioned this form of vehicular entertainment I held my breath, hoping my kids could appreciate something with a bit more edge than *The Sesame Street* soundtrack. When my preschool-aged son heard

Eddie's scorching "Eruption" solo for the first time, he exclaimed to me, all wide-eyed, "Daddy! That guitar . . . mean!" *Damn straight, son! And that sure kicks Radio Disney's ass.*

THE GETAWAY VEHICLE

It's taken a while, but I am slowly starting to accept the fact that until I win the lottery (not likely), master the art of selling short without a broker (even less likely), or my college band scores a recording contract (ha!), I'm just like every other schmuck whose bank account simply doesn't allow him the luxury of choosing a car that best matches the image he'd like to convey. To cheer up, I remind myself that at least I have something marginally hip to drive during those rare occasions when I'm not transporting the kids around. Without my Purple Rain I'd feel lost, normal, and, quite possibly, ordinary.

As a helmetless teenager navigating rural streets filled with scooter gangs, I never thought I'd join the other team and one day evolve into a full-fledged member of the suburban minivan parent posse. But now that I'm the owner of a lame-ass seven-passenger lemon, I've decided to make lemonade. And you can too, so long as you're able to secure your very own getaway vehicle—be it a convertible, a Harley, or a scooter—and fly away on a joyride of solitude and delusional dreaming that you're "other car" really isn't a minivan.

So I say thank God for my scooter! (Or should I say Kelly's scooter?) Now that our children are old enough to lock their little arms around my expanding waist, I look forward to every spring when I ignore that single-passenger warning sticker, and I take them for the first scoot of the season around our neighborhood. In fact, it's become something of a family tradition, a tradition I regretfully never experienced as a child. In the late 1950s, my dad owned a white MG two-seater convertible before he was married, and I always wished he had saved it for me and my brother and sister, never understanding how impractical that would prove. Now that I'm a parent, stealing away my children for a quick scooter ride reminds me of how lucky I am that I got my Purple Rain back and can pass it along to the fruit of my loins.

As we whisk around the neighborhood, I'm sure I look like an age-clueless fool—resembling one of those young, fun uncles much more than an aging, responsible father. But for those precious few moments, I stop caring about image, status, or sending messages to the world like "Easy!" "Quick!" "Fun!" or "Sexy!" Instead, I rev up the throttle, bite my kids' ears, and simply appreciate the sheer joy of sharing a ripping good time with my favorite grade-schoolers. In the end, that's what really moves me the most.

f us never planned o
his happening. But it di
ometime between gra
chool and our first mort
age, a strange phenom
non began replacing ou
outhful mojos with
ew-found maturity. An
e didn't see it coming
ur two-door coupe
orphed into sliding
oor minivans. Bar-hop
ng turned into movi
ghts on the couch. No
e write letters to th
itor. And golfa. It's n

8. HOME IMPROVEMENTS

Feeling Like a Tool

YOU KNOW THOSE WILD bachelor parties where guys treat their soon-to-be-married buddy to an evening of raucous partying, bottomless shot glasses, and endless lap dances? Neither do I.

But that's okay. When my best man James organized my bachelor party, his remarkably considerate goal was to leave me with something more than a hangover. His solution? A tool bash, where all the guests were required to bring me useful items to fill my tool box (assuming I had owned one).

So what did this accidental adult reap from his super-mature college buddies?

- **One sawhorse.** This is a contraption that typically requires a pair in order to stabilize your home repair project. One alone is about as useful as a single walkie-talkie. Thanks, Demps. You make me feel considerate.
- **A caulking gun.** You might think this was thoughtfully bestowed upon me so I could

> "The less you know sometimes, the better."
>
> — MacGyver

protect my home from crack and crevice intrusions like water, air, and insects. Nope. A buddy gave me a caulking gun for the purpose of providing a roomful of juvenile guys an excuse to enthusiastically repeat the word "caulk" in unison for the rest of the night. Thanks, Potter. You make me feel mature.

- **A can of WD-40.** Nothing funny about that, right? Fast forward to several months later when I gave up trying to correctly insert the precision spray straw into the nozzle, and I simply showered my squeaky door hinge with an uncontrolled blast that drenched much of the door frame and nearby wall. Turns out my friend Chuck had replaced the patented WD-40 straw with an average cocktail straw that couldn't possibly fit. He finally got his laugh when I left him a well-deserved voice mail message saying simply, "Good one, dickhead. You got me," confirming his success. Thanks, Chuck. You make me feel like . . . well, read on . . .

FEELING LIKE A TOOL

When it comes to home improvements, you could say the joke is still on me. Call me repair impaired. Or simply call me a fix-it failure. Just don't call me a do-it-yourselfer. Because when things go to hell around the house and repairs are required, at best I'm a do-it-*for*-me kind of guy who's craftiness and dexterity is a lot less like MacGyver and a lot more like the explosion-prone MacGruber.

To put it bluntly, home repairs usually make me feel like a tool.

Sure, I've had some marginal success crossing a few projects off the proverbial "Honey-Do" list. It's just that in my house, the list is usually titled, "Honey-*Don't*, Unless You Really Know What You're Doing This Time."

What could prompt such a stinging lack of confidence from my beloved life partner? I blame it on Kelly's mercilessly accurate long-term memory regarding a series of somewhat notorious events. Allow me to escort you through some of my most memorable fix-it foibles that belong in . . .

THE UNHANDY MAN'S HOME REPAIR HALL OF SHAME

THE DAY THE GARAGE DOOR WOULDN'T OPEN

Because we live in Minnesota, this misfortune happened in February of course, and it required immediate action. For me, that meant calling Chuck.

In my circle of amateur adult pals, Chuck is the least accidental of us adults largely because he knows his way around a skill saw. In fact, his expertise is so legendary, our mantra of awe has become, "That Chuck . . . he knows his stuff!"

So when Chuck arrived with his ten-pocket commercial-grade leather toolbelt firmly fastened around his waist, I breathed a sigh of relief. If anyone can fix this, Chuck could. Sure enough, a thirty-second diagnosis was followed by a swift repair as he effortlessly plugged in the garage door opener's power cord that had slipped out of the ceiling outlet. That Chuck . . . he knows his stuff!

THE NIGHT I PRIMED THE NURSERY WITH KILZ

Every pregnant wife deserves a handy husband to help her complete her nesting activities with success. Unfortunately for Kelly, she got stuck with me. Nothing says "I love you" to an expectant mother quite like priming her nursery walls with Kilz—a flammable oil-based primer—that's a noxious irritant and could cause respiratory tract inflammation when inhaled. Needless to say, I exhaled mightily once she left the house to sleep more safely at a friend's place that night.

THE BIRTHDAY BIKE I COULDN'T ASSEMBLE

Try telling a six-year-old birthday boy to demonstrate patience while you assemble his new bicycle. What was the hang up? I had nearly stripped the pedal assembly threads trying to screw on the left foot pedal. After finally giving up and throwing the bike (and my disappointed son) into the minivan, my favorite hardware store manager explained to us that the left pedal actually screws on in the opposite direction. Apparently one bicycle pedal must be reverse threaded so it doesn't fall off. Okay, I get that whole safety thing, but what ever happened to the age-old adage "righty-tighty, lefty-loosey"? Isn't that the universally accepted first lesson and absolute of home repairs? Is nothing sacred? To console myself for failing to try "lefty-tighty," I became convinced the manufacturer assembled the bike in a bizarre universe somewhere south of the equator where water circles down the drain counterclockwise, too.

THE DAY DADDY CUT THE CABLE TV
AND PHONE CORDS

No home improvement project is more deceivingly complicated than landscaping. Anybody can plant a tree or trim a hedge, right? Well, when it comes to digging shallow border trenches to position brick pavers around your house, take this advice: Before you dig, call your local utilities company for help locating the buried cables. When my compact ditch trencher sliced through the television cable—and minutes later, the telephone wire—my wife and children cared little about my own safety. Forget the fact that I could have electrocuted myself had I hit a power line. My family was livid because Daddy had just severed his family's communication lifelines to an outside, idyllic, escapist world—a fantasyland where real men take the time to figure out what they're doing before they start pushing a powerful lawn machine.

Clearly, society (and more importantly, my wife) values handiness and shuns incompetence. So what's an accidental adult to do? Over the years, I have cultivated a few tricks for faking my way through many a prickly project. These skills are certainly not foolproof, but they might help you patch up something more important than your drywall (think: marriage). And if you're really convincing, you might even dupe your neighbors into believing you welcome a good repair challenge. So try a few of these handy home improvement dos and don'ts, and maybe, just maybe, you can find a way to . . .

SURVIVE THE SCRUTINY: DOS AND DON'TS FOR THE REPAIR-IMPAIRED ACCIDENTAL ADULT

DO: ASSIGN BLAME FOR YOUR FAILURES

The key to avoiding criticism for screwing up home improvement projects is to deflect the responsibility at every opportunity. Simply swat away accountability like a pesky fly.

- **Blame the tools.** You have two choices here. Either you didn't have the appropriate tools for the job, or the tools themselves were faulty. Why didn't you have the right tools? Simple. You loaned them to a friend, because that's just the kind of guy you are. And why were the tools ruined? You see, good fathers let their children double as Daddy's little helpers. And sometimes your little fix-it friends leave a pair of vice grips out in the rain overnight, causing immediate and irreparable rusting, which, of course, renders them useless. Remember: inferior instruments equals unreliable repairs.

- **Blame the product packaging.** Those bastards shorted you again! Some assembly-line idiot can't count correctly, and now you're left holding the bag. How are you supposed to assemble a child's desk set when you need eight washer assemblies and they only gave you six? This was a setup from the start!
- **Blame the instruction manual.** Clearly, the technical writer assigned to this task does not speak (nor write) English as a first language. That means you're on your own deciphering their odd instruction-speak. When the project is failing as a result, tell your spouse, *I would be very appreciate much should their manual provide terrific instruction help support.*

DON'T: MISPLACE YOUR MATERIALS

As you tear open that glorious garbage-disposal box and prepare to install that three-quarter horsepower beauty, don't become so lost in the moment that the packaging goes flying, especially the instruction manual. I know many men who think that following the user's guide is unnecessary, lame, or "for wimps." Don't be deterred by this barbaric thinking. Sure, a lost set of instructions or a missing gasket gives you the ammunition you need to avoid responsibility (*see "Do: Blame the Product Packaging"*). But why make home repairs more difficult for yourself? Accidental adults need every advantage they can get.

DO: CUT YOURSELF

It might sound a little counterintuitive, but you'd be amazed at how much sympathy flows from a little blood. And remember, most bleeding is less severe than it appears. I'm not talking, "Hurry! Make a tourniquet!" All it takes is a quick poke of a tack or a carpet staple and you've just demonstrated the ultimate sacrifice of shedding blood for your feeble efforts. Want to extend the sympathy beyond the moment? Leave a few blood-stained tissues wet-side up in the bathroom waste basket as a visual reminder of your injury. And don't forget to wear a Band-Aid long after it's necessary.

DON'T: MAKE A BIG DEAL OVER A LITTLE REPAIR

So you fixed the storm door latch. Great. It probably feels like you scored a late-game touchdown, but try to act like you've been in the end zone before. Once after successfully installing a new garbage disposal, I blasted off an exuberant, self-congratulatory mass e-mail to all my buddies. Sure enough, my friend Chris replied (cc'ing all the guys), "Great job, Colin. By the way, was it really a new installation or, more accurately, a replacement?" Touché, my friend . . . or in this case, more like douché! Either way, I was busted. And deservedly so. I should've known better.

DO: "CHUCK" IT

Whenever a project is worth a proper repair that I can't provide, I "Chuck" it. No I don't throw it away. Instead, I pick up the phone and call my friend Chuck who's more than willing to help. When you're in the same boat, I encourage you to find your own Chuck and do the same. Just leave mine alone. He's busy.

DON'T: CHUCK IT

This is the more commonly used "chuck it," and it refers to tossing a seemingly unfixable item—while uttering a phrase that rhymes with "chuck it." But don't give up so easily. Instead, sell your broken possessions on Craigslist or eBay. You may be surprised by how many people are interested in collecting crap. (You've already met my friend Brian.)

DO: LEARN THE NAMES OF YOUR TOOLS

Believe me, I know it's much easier to ask your wife to bring you "that pointy metal thing with the orange handle." But you'll impress her mightily if you call for the needle-nose pliers. When she asks you to just describe the tool because she doesn't know the proper names as well as you, offer up an exasperated, dramatic sigh and relent. Little does she know that before you asked for her assistance, you racked your brain for five minutes trying to remember the name of that tool you silently think of as "that pointy metal thing with the orange handle."

DON'T: DISRESPECT THE HARDWARE STORE STAFF

Sure, the word "ballcock" is funny. But the guy working the plumbing aisle stopped laughing long ago when accidental adults like you snicker as you ask for help finding one. Same with the guy in the flooring section who exasperatedly explains to you, "It's called 'tounge *and* groove,' not 'tongue *in* groove.'" Piss these guys off, and you'd better save your receipts because you're SOL if you're left navigating the store on your own, attempting to find the right materials you need. And if you're embarrassed about (or banned from) asking for help, bring your own "Chuck" with you. He'll know where to locate the ballcocks and stud finders, 'cause, you know, that Chuck . . . .

DO: VIE FOR PRIVACY

In a perfect world, unhandy accidental adults would get the house to themselves whenever embarking on a messy and lengthy home improvement project. Cutting ceramic tiles with a wet saw in the garage until 2 A.M. probably wasn't my most neighborly move ever, but the freedom of having the house (and the weekend) to myself was quite liberating. Because this scenario doesn't happen very often, it's up to you to set some expectations. Tell your wife she can stick around and watch the systematic, yet temporary, destruction of her home while you set about to improve it—or she can grab the kids and get the hell out of Dodge, treating herself to a more peaceful weekend at a relative's house. Don't be surprised when neither option sounds particularly enticing to her. If she chooses to stay, just remind her she's about to see how sausage is made, and it ain't pretty.

DON'T: ATTRACT A CROWD

Want to complicate an already plagued project? Add a little performance anxiety! Try erecting a six-sided modular redwood playground set (with faulty tools and confusing instructions) while the neighbors watch the debacle unfold on your lawn in stunned disbelief. Instead, whenever possible, assemble projects under the cover of darkness in the garage with the door closed. This setup will also muffle the inevitable obscenities that will flow.

DO: BUY YOURSELF TIME

One of the most reasonable yet feared questions ever asked of an accidental adult is "Honey, how long will your project take?" No matter what the do-it-yourself assembly guide says, provide your wife with an approximation that is twice as long as the experts estimate. "Um, the manual says to expect six hours. I think I can do that." This way, when that three-hour project pushes you to twelve hours, you can tell your livid wife that most projects realistically take twice as long as expected. Be sure to consider these timesavers as well:

- Before you begin, fuel your vehicle with a full tank of gas for those hourly trips to Home Depot.
- Plan on eating all meals behind the wheel.
- Limit your liquid intake to reduce trips to the bathroom, which tend to leave paint-stained footprints on the rug.
- Music makes any job easier, so create your iPod "Fix-it" mix the night before a major repair, not in the middle of the project.

DON'T: BUY WHEN YOU CAN BORROW

Sure that shiny orange smart-start chain saw looks enticing. And, yes, that 4,000 psi pressure washer would be a great addition to your collection of unkempt tools strewn about the garage. But really, how often do you have to fell a tree or deep-clean your siding by blasting it with four gallons of water per minute? If you're like me, maybe once every leap year. So put away your credit card, and call your more mature neighbor who already owns these tools and demonstrates more responsibility than you would by keeping them clean, organized, and in good working order. The unspoken rental fee in my neighborhood is quite reasonable—it's usually a six-pack of beer and the understanding that you'll return a wheelbarrow spotless, despite a little known fact overlooked by the majority of my immaculate garage-owning neighbors: *wheelbarrows were designed to carry dirt.*

DO: VOLUNTEER TO HELP YOUR FRIENDS

This tactic benefits you twofold. First off, if you help your friends with their projects, they will pay you back. And that's about the only way you'll accomplish any significant improvement or repair projects at your own home. (Also, if you don't already have a friend like Chuck, do whatever it takes to befriend one immediately.) Secondly, as your wife and neighbors watch you load up your toolbox and pull out of the driveway, they'll think you're a saint for offering your assistance to buddies who could use the help. Then when you arrive at your buddy's backyard deck-building party, volunteer to be the one who goes on that inconvenient Home Depot run. Rushing out to pick up a few more boxes of lag screws keeps you from revealing your ineptitude back at the construction site. Otherwise you're stuck fetching tools for your friends and trying to stay out of their way.

DON'T: DISREGARD THE LAW

Despite the accidental adult's characteristic disregard for convention, there's a time and a place for paying attention to the rules. The time? Whenever your project is so prolonged that it would really suck to have to tear it down, make it three feet narrower, and erect it again. The place? Your backyard. So here are some words to familiarize yourself with: ordinances, codes, permits, setbacks, zones, variances. Local building inspectors are a lot like those C-shift security officers—a little bit of authority gives them just enough juice to become tyrants who love nothing more than handing out violations.

But their infuriating rules provide no justification for becoming a scofflaw. Pulling a permit before you start a project is better than pulling your hair out later.

DO: PLAY THE "YOU CAN'T FIX IT EITHER!" CARD

Use this one sparingly, as it can lead to long-term marital resentment. But when all else fails, and she backs you against a wall, simply remind your wife she's even less adept than you. So if you can't fix it, she certainly can't, either. In this way, your incompetence is her fault. I mean, she knew she was marrying an unhandy man, didn't she?

DON'T: THROW AWAY RECEIPTS

Face it. The chances of you purchasing the exact amount of materials necessary for your project, let alone the correct materials, are slim to none. That's why it's helpful to save all your receipts. My filing system (stuffing handfuls of crumpled slips into a cigar box) isn't the envy of the neighborhood, but it's one step better than digging through garbage cans looking for discarded receipts stuck at the bottom. With proof of payment in hand, you'll find that zipping through the return register saves you time so you can re-enter the store and purchase more supplies in incorrect quantities that you'll return later, if you so choose. (You really can never have enough spackle.)

LIKE FATHER, (NOT) LIKE SON

Like many sons, I was convinced my father knew how to perform every home improvement task possible. No project ever seemed to fluster him, stump him, or ultimately beat him. Fortunately for my dad, my older brother soaked up his skills, and today Ryan can disassemble and reassemble his 1000cc Italian superbike motorcycle and end up with no spare parts left over (though I refuse to accept a ride with him until he recognizes my scooter as a worthy road partner).

Now that I'm a father, I wonder what my son will think of me as he watches me grunt, struggle, sweat, and sometimes give up when the repair becomes too challenging. I pray I've got a few more years before his cerebrum fully develops and he concludes I'm a fraud.

But if I ultimately can't demonstrate the wisest path to handiness, maybe at least I can show him (and you) the smartest route to revenge. Consider this trick the next time you need to zing somebody, accidental-adult style.

Years after my tool-themed bachelor party, I exacted revenge on Chuck for giving me that trick can of WD-40. At his bachelor party, I proudly gave him a window insulation kit for winterizing his home. Each prepackaged kit includes shrinkable film sheets and a roll of tape—double-sided so the film would adhere to the sill. When winter approached several months later, Chuck discovered in midproject that his special kit was not tamper-proofed because *his* came with several shrinkable film sheets and a roll of *single-sided* tape.

Yes, that Colin . . . he knows his stuff!

And you can too. All it really takes to navigate the world of home improvements is to know your limitations before you get in over your head. And since most accidental adults tend to be keenly aware of their shortcomings, this should pose little difficulty. Once you've identified a project that's beyond your capacity, ramp up that inner monologue and remind yourself that even the handiest of men get stumped from time to time. So you're no Bob Villa. But you're also no fool. You're an accidental adult. And when it comes to projects that *really* matter (like replacing dead batteries in your beloved remote control), you know your stuff.

f us never planned o
his happening. But it di
ometime between gra
chool and our first mort
age, a strange phenom
non began replacing ou
outhful mojos with
ew-found maturity. An
e didn't see it comin
ur two-door coupe
orphed into sliding
oor minivans. Bar-hop
ing turned into mov
ghts on the couch. No
e write letters to th

9. CIVIC DUTIES

Caring So Little about So Much

IN THE UNIQUE LEXICON of the typically ambivalent accidental adult, it's hardly a secret that our favorite words happen to be *carefree, irresponsible*, and, my personal favorite, *optional*. Conversely, it stands to reason that words like *duty, responsibility*, and *obligation* typically arouse disdain and, ultimately, great personal discomfort.

Sadly, these and any other words that invoke a particular requirement also provide a harsh reminder of the reality so many of us accidental adults would prefer to ignore: Society does not provide accidental adults shelter or exemption from observing the same set of civic responsibilities required of assimilated adults. (Sucks, I know.) These duties typically include paying taxes, registering for military service, obeying the law, and voting. When you consider that failure to perform three of those four responsibilities can land you behind bars, society's message becomes clear: Be a good citizen, do the right thing, and enjoy your freedom in return. But as bothersome as most

"I marched at peace rallies. It wasn't so much because of my great love of peace as it was because of my great love of female companionship."

—Jesse Ventura, *I Ain't Got Time to Bleed*

obligations can seem, there is another civic responsibility that oddly plays to the strengths of the accidental adult. And sooner or later this duty comes calling, and we all will likely get our chance to play the role of Good Citizen.

YOU'VE GOT MAIL

I'll bet most people you know probably consider a jury summons something akin to a death sentence sealed in an envelope. And why wouldn't they? Selection to serve the judicial branch of government translates into lost days from work, the possibility of reduced income, and interminable waiting. And waiting. And then some more waiting.

Then there are us accidental adults who count ourselves among the very few people who have actually aspired to perform jury duty. And why wouldn't we? Jury duty provides a rare opportunity to demonstrate two of our most frequently exercised skills at the same time: pretending to be high-functioning members of the adult world and casting judgments on others. A perfect combo!

When I got my summons in the mail, I actually cheered. For me, it meant more than just performing my civic duty. As a writer, I had always dreamed of the chance to serve on some groundbreaking legal thriller and then rat on my fellow jurors in a best-selling behind-the-scenes tell-all.

My elation was quickly tempered when I began to realize my chances of actually serving on a jury were slim to none.

A JURY OF WHOSE PEERS?

"You'll never get picked," my boss informed me. "They don't want people like you . . . young, educated, creative thinker, professional."

Of course, those were all compliments, but I really hoped she was wrong. If she were right, what would that say about "a jury of your peers"? And worse, what would it say if I *did* get selected? The attorneys think I'm dim? Easily manipulated? An ordinary adult? Good God, no!

Now I was beginning to think those real-world adults understood something I didn't. Maybe considering a jury summons a stroke of good luck actually just made me a stroke.

Skipping out on jury duty is a misdemeanor in Minnesota (I looked into it), so I really had no choice. If Lady Justice pointed her finger at me, then so be it. Every statue I've seen of her shows a woman wearing a blindfold. So I must have a fifty-fifty chance of getting on a case anyway, right?

And after watching the mandatory video the morning I reported, my chances didn't look half bad. Granted, the orientation video— *All Rise: Jury Service in Minnesota*—was bad. Like, cheesy bad. (The acting being just slightly better than porn, or so I'd imagine.) But I snapped to attention when I heard: "Some members of the jury panel will be excused from serving on the jury." The video continued, "If you are excused, do not take offense. It doesn't mean that anyone doubts that you are a *fair* and a *good* person."

I still had a chance. But what would it mean if I *was* dismissed from jury selection? The video didn't explain, but the cynic in me had a few ideas.

Free Legal Advice—What Jury Selection Rejection Really Means!

Before you can judge a case involving strangers and lawyers, strange lawyers will judge you. So who's on trial anyway?

The judge will ask you to be impartial, but the attorneys really would prefer you to be persuadable. Nice cooperation guys.

In the event that you fail to demonstrate either impartiality or resistance to persuasion, you will be excused and sent back to the assembly room to await another trial calling for a jury. Hey, you still might be good enough for someone!

Your reputation for being a fair and good person can remain intact at least in the eyes of the judicial system, which is technically blind. So when you get teased for being excused from a trial, politely inform everyone, "The courts said you shouldn't doubt that I am a fair and good person." If necessary, add a "So screw you!" at the end of your retort for emphasis.

After being excused, somehow find a way to consider it a compliment and not a rejection. Describe your peers who were ultimately seated on the jury as rejects from the Deliverance *casting call for locals, and your friends should get the idea (at least the ones who've seen the film).*

CALL OF DUTY

The jury selection process is a waiting game. The "will I or won't I" get picked (or not) is enough to drive a guy insane. When you get the tap to serve, you'd better be prepared . . . to sit around. The idiosyncrasies of your fellow citizens will only entertain so much.

MONDAY, DAY 1

"Please take a seat and prepare to wait for the next five days."

Those are the instructions I hear—or something like that. The jury assembly room looks like something out of the bar scene in

Star Wars. Imagine 100 humorless people from assorted backgrounds jammed into a room, held against their will, knowing they're about to be bored stiff. Wading through the group, I decide to find a seat across from the most attractive and presumably best-smelling citizens I can find. That way, when I look up from my newspaper, I might share an "oh-man-I-feel-your-pain!" look with someone affable.

So I settle in across from a thirtysomething woman who's wearing her hair braided in pigtails. Odd styling choice I think, but she's pretty enough. One seat away from her is a somewhat timid-looking and blonde college-aged girl who's attracting some not-so-subtle ogling from a majority of the men in the room. But not from me. Nope. I've come prepared with three newspapers, a short John Steinbeck novel, and a book of crossword puzzles to hold my attention . . . unlike the sulking, all denim-wearing guy three rows behind me. When I turn around to hear the instructions from the jury manager, I catch a glimpse of this Sulking Denim Guy, staring off into space. No books, no magazines, no conversation with others. Just sitting there, literally . . . doing . . . nothing. I've rarely seen such a display of static emptiness. It's a little creepy and fascinating all at the same time.

"Thank you for serving as potential jurors," the jury manager says, as if we had a choice. (Did I mention that misdemeanor thing?) "I'd like to go over a few of the guidelines and expectations."

As I listen to his litany of rules, which aren't so few, the following stand out.

"No gum chewing in the courtroom."

For an average adult, this wouldn't be a problem. But for an accidental adult like me, gum chewing is a hobby. And it never hurts to have fresh breath, especially when you're sitting across from Cute College Girl. Fine. I can live without it.

"Do not drink alcoholic beverages during trial breaks."
An audible groan from Sulking Denim Guy. Hey, it's alive!

"If at all possible, you will be dismissed for the day if our courts tell me they do not need any more jurors."
Hmmm. Would I go back to work? Go home? Or steal a few precious moments browsing the drum room at Guitar Center? So many choices . . . .

As this first morning drags on, I sail through my newspapers and a third of my Steinbeck paperback without getting called to a courtroom. I take no offense, although I am slightly saddened that Cute College Girl got called to a courtroom, leaving me behind. I'll miss her quiet beauty. But mostly her quiet. By now, many prospective jurors are getting chummy with each other and passing the time with small talk. This includes Pigtail Woman, who has made friends with another woman in our little section of the assembly room, and they're chatting a little too loudly for this introvert. I try to tune them out, but it doesn't really matter. By midafternoon, the original 100 has been pared to about fifty of us remaining, and by late afternoon, we, the unchosen, are dismissed for the day.

It's Guitar Center time!

TUESDAY, DAY 2

It's 5:30 A.M., and Kelly nudges me in bed. "I've been pretty sick all night. Can you pleeeeeeease try to get a sick day and help with the kids at home today?" she moans.

Getting excused from jury duty turns out to be a bit easier than I had imagined. It helps that I haven't been seated on a trial. It also helps, I suspect, that the jury manager has heard more lame illness excuses than an HR director on the Friday before Memorial Day weekend. So when I call and explain my situation to him, he's more than prepared with an answer.

"Sorry to hear that, Colin. Go ahead and take the day off, but please report again tomorrow morning. If you can't, that's fine. Your name goes back into the pool, and you'll have to repeat your service another week, sometime soon."

I pray it's a twenty-four-hour bug.

WEDNESDAY, DAY 3

Good news! It was a twenty-four-hour bug! So armed with my supply of newspapers and crosswords, I settle into my little corner of the assembly room. As the others gather, I see Cute College Girl has returned, dismissed from a previous trial. Sulking Denim Guy is there as well, motionless, vacant, and looking as though he might have slept in the chair overnight. Pigtail Woman has changed her hairstyle, but I still recognize her voice as she again holds court with her friend in another section of the room. But not for long. We're dismissed for the day before noon! Thirty jubilant jurors rush the door.

THURSDAY, DAY 4

Another three-newspaper morning and an alcohol-free lunch (of course). But today, I finally get the call to a courtroom. Here we go! Game time! I'm ready to play an indispensable role in our justice system.

After the jury manager calls the names of us chosen few, we're led upstairs to a dark and musty courtroom that's much smaller than I would have imagined. There's twenty-nine of us filing into the gallery benches in the back, and the bailiff encourages us to continue squeezing in like lemmings. At the council table facing us we meet the prosecuting attorney, the defense attorney, and the defendant.

Who says stereotypes are inaccurate and unfounded? To challenge that premise, please allow me to now pre-judge our cast of characters for you—fully acknowledging that none of these conclusions is based on one shred of evidence presented.

The presiding judge: Way out of our league. Elderly, wise, succinct, and very aware of his intimidating nature. Doesn't appear to suffer fools gladly.

The charge? Order in the court.

My verdict? *Thy will be done.*

Prosecuting attorney: Straight out of central casting. Handsome, charming, confident, and quick with a smile. Expensive suit, shiny shoes, and sharp haircut.

The charge? The "burden of proof" is his.

My verdict? *No burden to him. He'll deliver.*

Defense attorney: Fresh out of law school. Green. Probably court-appointed. Sincere, deliberate, cautious, nervous. Wearing what looks like a T.J. Maxx sport coat I tried on last year.

The charge? Defending his client.

My verdict? *Prosecuting attorney will eat him for lunch.*

Defendant: Right outta Juvie Hall. No eye contact with jurors. Shifting, slumping, scowling . . . pissed off. No tie, no sport coat, no self-awareness.

The charge? Burglary.

My verdict? *Guilty . . . of not getting better body language advice from his attorney.*

Within minutes of entering and addressing the panel, the judge explains he needs to cut our group down to twelve jurors and one alternate. His first order of business? Dismissing his first juror— Cute College Girl. Turns out she recognizes the defendant from her high school. She's zero-for-two on juries this week. My opinion of her rises. Shortly thereafter, Sulking Denim Guy musters up some energy and announces that he's just spent the last four days sitting in an assembly room—get this—doing nothing. Whose fault is that? He then informs Hizzoner that he considers jury service a cruel form of punishment. Many of us would probably agree with him, but more than anyone confined to our holding room, he's clearly demonstrated this opinion daily with his zombielike behavior. Big surprise: the judge dismisses him, too.

The rest of the jury selection process isn't quite as speedy. One by one, each of us is called to take a seat in the jury box where we're asked to deliver a monologue on our background and life experiences. The judge instructs us to hit all the basics, or he'll follow up and pry it out. It sounds a little bit like those speed dating events, but with no promise of a happy ending.

"What's your name? Age? Where did you grow up? What did your parents do? Did you go to college? Where? Any graduate work? Where? Where do you live now? Your occupation? Married? Any kids? What does your spouse do? What do your children do? Do you have any brothers and sisters? What do they do?"

More Free Legal Advice for Accidental Adults!

If your goal is to get picked for jury service, then when it's your turn to share your abbreviated life story with a judge, a potential jury, and a small audience of legal practitioners, it's bad form to answer the question of, "What do you want to do with your life?" by singing that response from the Twisted Sister video, "I wanna' rock!" Strive to ignore your inner seventeen-year-old (for once) and instead summon up the maturity expected of legitimate grownups and give the court your spiel. Believe me, I know it's tough, but try to play along.

When it was my turn to share my tale, I begin by telling the judge I grew up in Wisconsin. He quickly interrupts me.

"From Wisconsin? Are you from the entire state, or any city in particular?" he chides.

Damn! I'm already blowing it.

"Sorry, your honor. I'm from Marshfield," I reply, trying my best to perform the part of an adult. But that act quickly fades. "So that makes me a Green Bay Packers fan," I find myself continuing, lapsing back into my juvenile safe harbor. "Would that excuse me from jury duty in this state?"

Fortunately for me, the judge has a slight sense of humor, although my fellow jurors seem to find this attempt at dismissal more admirable. He chuckles a bit, so I continue with my none-too-riveting life story.

Once each of us finishes our performances, the judge then begins a group interview process, telling us he's about to ask some questions that may be very personal and can be difficult to answer. A few jurors turn ashen, and rightly so. Think about it. Try baring your soul or explaining that youthful but sort of illegal indiscretion to a few dozen complete strangers, two lawyers, a defendant, a bailiff, and an intimidating judge. Good thing I've led a fairly vanilla life. The others? Not so much.

After hearing about assorted DWIs, hurled pop cans at police cars, and other legal run-ins, the judge asks us to raise our hand if any of his next questions apply. My hands remain at my lap as he shoots off his inquiries, but my inner smart-ass ramps up as usual.

Judge: "Have you ever been the victim of a crime?"

Inner monologue: *That bartender in Italy who charged me the equivalent of $15 for a bottle of beer victimized me pretty badly. But when in Rome . . .*

Judge: "Do you know any police officers or lawyers?"

Inner monologue: *Doesn't everybody? Great. We're going to be here all frickin' night.*

Judge: "Do you watch television shows like *CSI* or *Law and Order?*"

Inner monologue: *Nope, but I watch* Lost *where the castaways mete out their own warped brand of island justice. Does that count?*

Then the questions get a little more challenging. "Do you think the testimony of a police officer should always be considered credible?" No one raises a hand. "Does anyone disagree that the burden of proof lies with the state?" No one raises a hand. "Does anyone disagree that the defendant who sits here today is presumed innocent of the charges?" Nope. We all agree by law he's innocent (so far). "Would anyone be concerned if the defense never presents a case, or if the defendant never testifies on his behalf?"

Now he's got me. I think about this one for a second, and slowly my arm goes up. So does another person's—a corporate MBA woman who I suspect was intentionally trying to get dismissed. But that's it. Just the two of us. The judge pounces on her first, and when she explains her reasoning, she basically takes what would've been my explanation with responses like, "I don't have the facts yet, but I'd like to hear from the defendant," and "It might seem odd to only hear the prosecution's side." So when it's my turn to respond, about all I can offer is a profound, "It's like she said." Judge McTough reminds me that the defense is not required to say a word. I tell him I understand that. He asks me if I think I can be a fair and impartial juror without hearing from the defense. I give him a qualified, "I think I can." And finally helping me—a guy who uses words for a living but who is suddenly rendered inarticulate (damn MBA Woman had to go first!)—the judge generously offers, "It's just that . . . that . . . well . . . you would like to hear both sides of the story, is that it?" "Yes! That *is* it! It's just that I would like to hear both sides of the story!" I repeat.

The truth is, that really *was* it. Nothing more, nothing less. Maybe it's a result of my grad school years spent teaching undergrads to always present at least two sides of an argument in their speeches. Or maybe it's my knack for finding merits in both perspectives to an issue, which leaves me riding the fence on more topics than I'd like to admit.

But with that simple admission—that I wanted to hear both sides of the story—my "essential role in the American system of justice" came to a screeching halt. I just didn't know it yet.

When the judge finishes his questions, he turns it over to the lawyers. The prosecuting attorney suggests with an exasperated smile that he's tired (hey, he's just like us!), and he's had enough for one day.

He jokes to the jury, "What time is *Grey's Anatomy* on tonight?" He has no further questions for the jury. But not the defense attorney. No sirree! Checking his long list of notes, he methodically questions and requestions those who raised red flags for him. Like the judge before him, he asks MBA Woman why she would be concerned if the defense did nothing. Her answers don't change. I prepare to be interrogated the same, but he moves on. No questions for me. Doesn't even throw me a bone. His mind was made up. And that's when I knew my service was really over.

Minutes later, the attorneys agree on a slate of jurors and hand a list to the judge who reads off the names of those who would comprise the jury. Again, we're reminded not to take offense if not chosen.

Needless to say, "Colin Sokolowski" was not on the list.

Standing in the hallway outside the courtroom with the other rejects, I'm feeling a bit like that pretend adult again—trying to live in a world of real grownups "who get it." Then I'm reminded of that passage, "Many are called, but few are chosen." So I begin to take stock of who else filled the hallway. Among the castoffs, we have MBA Woman (big shock), an attorney (bigger shock), an international businessperson, and a game warden in training. Yes. Taking my own advice, I decide to consider this esteemed company. Esteemed company indeed.

The court clerk interrupts my internal rationalization by thanking us all and instructing us that we do not need to appear for jury duty tomorrow. Our service has concluded.

FRIDAY (OR DAY 5 FOR THE CHOSEN FEW)

When I returned to work the next morning, I walked the halls, sharing the details of my legal misadventure with anyone who would ask. To make me feel better, a coworker told me most juries look like the first twelve people you run into in a Wal-Mart on a Saturday morning. My boss was a bit more diplomatic.

"You know, it's not a popularity contest," she explained. "But knowing who's out there, I'd want you on my jury any day."

She may have just been propping me up, sensing I was sporting a slightly bruised ego. But I didn't care. What she said helped provide some closure to what was a long, sometimes boring, sometimes exciting, but always educational week, all rolled into one. And I knew what was really behind her words. Given all the evidence I had presented, she rendered her verdict. She did not doubt that I am a fair and good person.

JURY DUTY: LET'S GET OFF!

So what have I learned from my experience? Apparently if your goal is to *not* get picked for jury duty, you need to act like an accidental adult at every opportunity. (Shouldn't be difficult.) The following tactics will help you accomplish this amazingly simple goal.

1. Assume for a minute, as I do, that most lawyers don't want jurists who appear sharp enough to question their arguments or challenge their assumptions. If true, then the quickest route to the door is to dress like an intelligent, working professional. I know it's a day off of work and you paid a fortune for those relaxed bootleg Lucky brand jeans, but go for that corporate look over comfort. Remember, you can't impress your coworkers with your fashion sense on Casual Friday if you're sitting in a courtroom stuck on a jury.

2. A favorite college professor of mine once instructed us, "Just tell the court that you're a journalism student. That will scare the hell out of them." I only used this bit of bravado

once, when complaining about my hometown newspaper's decision to recap a Milwaukee Brewers game on the front of the sports page and burying their story about the NBA Finals game featuring my beloved Los Angeles Lakers on page three. Hopefully a judge will hold your journalism studies in higher regard than that sports page editor did, who painfully reminded me that, like all of his readers, I lived in Wisconsin, not California.

3. Establish credibility with the attorneys by telling them you know a sure-fire way you could pass the bar exam on your first attempt, if you really wanted to.

    Step 1: Eat exam.

    Step 2: Wait twelve hours.

    Step 3: Pass exam.

4. You know those people who use your name repeatedly in conversations, even though they've just met you? "You know, Mark, I think that's a great idea. I've been thinking a lot about this, Mark, and you're just the person we need to lead our efforts. Don't you think, Mark?" On the surface it might seem polite and familiar, yet deep down it really just smacks of condescension. So why not try this out on your new legal friends? After hearing his name used five times in every answer you offer, Counselor Cronberg might tire of your smug conceit just enough to cross you off his list.

5. Promise the court that ever since graduate school (red flag!), you're not that same guy who used to be able to blow a 0.8 by 8 A.M. most days. And assure them that you have no criminal history. In this country. But you also might warn them that ever since legislation passed making the environmentally friendly (but timid) 1.6 gallon toilets the law of the land, you now have joined a growing number of Americans

plotting ways to smuggle 3.5 gallon-per-flush toilets over the Canadian border. Because nothing strikes more fear in the heart of the U.S. legal system than bad asses who conspire with the ruthless Canadian Toilet Cartel.

ENGAGEMENT VERSUS ENRAGEMENT

Becoming a decent, upright, (somewhat) functioning member of society might feel a bit like selling out at times. But like it or not, the transformation does happen sooner or later to accidental and assimilated adults alike. When it does, you might just surprise yourself at how engaged you can become if the proper motivation presents itself (think: personal satisfaction).

- You might find yourself paying better attention to your property tax statements after an adult friend (who really cares about these tedious matters) points out that your county raised your taxes at a higher rate than your neighbors. My response to this indignation wasn't particularly productive—"I don't like this, so this sucks, and that means I am right, and the county is wrong, and everyone can bite me!"—but at least I felt the brief intoxication of civic engagement that some adults have droned about.
- You might find yourself voting faithfully in every election. But in true accidental adult fashion, you might vote for candidates based on their photogenic qualities (or of their spouses'), rather than their positions on the issues. Hey, it's your vote. Who am I to argue? I once cast my ballot for a U.S. senate candidate because his wife was killer attractive, a working actress/model, and she often appeared on TV. (Six more years!)

- You might even find yourself caring enough about your community that you will actually attempt to improve it. I did when I embarked on an ultimately ill-fated campaign to retrofit my already fully developed subdivision with sidewalks so my family and I could finally take walks and bike rides in safety. Unfortunately my brilliant proposal was rejected by a vocal minority of the subdivision who thought the perfect location for such an amenity was on the opposite side of their street. Out of spite to this personal slight, I now tell my children to go ahead and walk through their lawns. "Feel free to drag your heels!"

It's natural to feel that civic engagement can too quickly lead to civic enragement simply because society is expecting you to embrace responsibility and contribute to the cause. But to be fair (and somewhat adult) for one fleeting moment, I've found that doing the right thing and performing your civic responsibilities is merely the small price we pay for living among the grownups. Taxes? Yes, they suck, but cheating the system isn't fair to accidental adults because we don't know your tricks. Registering for military service? If our fathers did it, why shouldn't we? (I'm clearly no better than my dad.) Obeying the law? I typically don't like the consequences of ignoring this one. Voting? Whose mug do you want to see every night on the news? Choose wisely! And jury duty? Judging others just plain feels good sometimes.

So whatever the request, when you hear your country's call to service, do the right thing (for once), play adult, and don't let it bounce over to voice mail. If you try that move once too often, your objection will be overruled.

Court adjourned.

f us never planned o
his happening. But it di
ometime between gra
chool and our first mort
age, a strange phenom
non began replacing ou
outhful mojos with
ew-found maturity. An
e didn't see it coming
ur two-door coupe
orphed into sliding
oor minivans. Bar-hop
ng turned into movi
ghts on the couch. Nov
e write letters to th
itor. And golfe. It's n

10. ATHLETICS

Putting the Beer in Beer League

YOU KNOW THE KID from grade school who was picked last in gym class? Or the one who dropped the easy fly ball in centerfield that led to the scoring run? Or the boy the other team fouled in youth basketball league because sending him to the free-throw line meant enjoying a good rest and getting the ball back with no threat of two points added to the score board? That would be me, laughing all the way. Believe me when I say I really couldn't care less. Sure, earning a solid reputation in sports never hurts a boy's self-esteem. But my route to recognition was always plotted through the demonstration of musical talent, not athletic ability. Don't rock 'n' roll gods attract more groupies than sports stars? Unlike most boys my age, I was determined to win admiration with drumsticks, not hockey sticks.

Now that I'm older, I still don't care much about my athletic ability, as evidenced by my preference for recreation and my disdain for competition. The reality is many accidental adults just don't give a damn

> "It just doesn't matter if we win or if we lose. It just doesn't matter! It just doesn't matter!"
>
> —Tripper Harrison, *Meatballs*

about their own personal performance in sports. To do so would be, well . . . adultlike. And that's not our game. Unless by accident (of course) we discover we might actually be adequate or better at a particular sport, as I learned some years ago.

SHOCK ABSORBING

"Dude, I didn't know you were fast!"

My buddy Brian was impressed when I recalled one of my recent race results over happy hour miniburgers a few summers ago. Coming from a guy who dabbled in running for about a decade, his pronouncement made me think maybe I'm onto something. That and it was about the first athletically related compliment I had received from anyone other than my mother.

With the exception of high school tennis, which doesn't exactly qualify me for super-jock status, I had never in my life met a sport that agreed with me. So imagine my surprise when decades after the teen years, I have finally discovered a genuine adult athletic activity I'm actually decent at: long-distance running. And it took a fair bit of convincing before I was willing to admit that I might be a little bit stronger than your average headband-wearing, wheezing weekend runner.

I had only recently started running casually, so naturally Brian's observation took me by surprise. Why ? Because the real adult world places an unnecessary emphasis on physical prowess and athletic competition. Too many people take sports, which is nothing more than a series of games and activities, way too seriously. Need proof? Then consider the stark differences between assimilated adults and accidental adults when it comes to athletics:

- Most accidental adults don't drive golf balls 300 yards down the center of the fairway and remark, "Topped it a little, but I think it's going to bump and run nicely." Nope. You smack the shit out of your nudie golf tee, sending the ball skimming twenty-five yards into the rough and grab another beer from the cooler in the cart.

- When you decide to join the company softball team, you become unnerved and confused to learn that opposing teams no longer lob easy-to-hit pitches like they did in your college beer league. Instead, a cutthroat pitcher now has the balls to attempt to strike you out. This guy would rather take you on one-on-one than involve his other eight teammates in the action. (There's no *i* in "team," but you clearly can't spell "pitcher" without one.)

- When someone tosses out the neon yellow Nerf football to liven up the backyard party, no matter how many times you throw a perfect spiral, that one time you loft a wobbling wounded duck (and blame it on those damn squishy foam balls that are impossible to control), it's ADULT MALE TO THE RESCUE! "You know, if you just move your pinky to the fourth slot between the laces, you'll tighten that spiral every time." Thanks man. Your life-changing advice was so critical to my enjoyment of this little game of catch.

Yet quite by accident, hidden beneath my unimposing, reluctant-adult exterior, was a somewhat promising athlete (of sorts)—an adequate runner equipped with some startling endurance and surprising confidence. More shocking than that, I also discovered I possessed an innate desire to run, an urge to run, a . . . (wait for it) . . . passion to run.

JOINING THE TEAM

It seems no matter what, assimilated adults will seize any opportunity they can find to ruin a fun activity by moving it from recreation to competition. And always the pessimist, I predicted that an impending threat of competition would soon accompany my new-found pastime. So naturally, my heart skipped a beat when after dispensing his surprising praise, Brian suggested I kick it up a notch. Or so I thought.

"Let's run a race together," he suggested. "There's this great 5K race in downtown Minneapolis at night. It'll be great. And plenty of eye candy there too, if you know what I mean."

When it comes to deciphering sexually suggestive commentary, it's pretty easy to pick up on what Brian means. But the invitation still left me confused.

"What do you mean, 'run a race together'?" I needed to know. "You want to keep the same pace, or just enter together and we'll meet up at the finish line?"

"Relax," he assured me. "I just think it would be fun to run the same race together. We'll each do our own thing. You'll smoke me anyway. We'll have some laughs and a few beers afterwards."

"Sorry," I apologized. "I'm not usually invited to do something athletic. I'm a bit out of my element here."

It was true. Aside from an annual outing of golf (which I still contend is a game much like billiards and bowling and not a sport), I'm not too familiar with doing the buddy/sport thing. The buddy/drinking thing? Yes. The buddy/rock concert thing? Love it. The buddy/I'll-bet-our-server-thinks-I'm-cuter-than-you-are-competition thing? One of my favorites. But the buddy/sport thing? Foreign territory.

I should have known Brian wasn't like those other super-serious, real adults who always need to keep score against you. After all, this was the guy who at age twenty (and a 5' 7", 125-pound build) auditioned to compete as a contestant on *American Gladiators* with our friend James just for a good laugh. (They were both summarily dismissed within a few ticks of the preliminary fitness test, which required contestants to perform twenty chin-ups in less than thirty seconds. They were laughing too hard to even finish ten. Next!)

So quite casually, Brian and I ran "together." Which means he and I registered together, collected our postrace free drink tickets *together*, joined the other runners stretching out on the sidewalks and enjoyed that scenery *together*, headed to the starting line *together*, and after finishing about two minutes apart met up past the finish line *together*. I have to admit, the buddy/sport thing really was fun. And by running hard, doing well, and posting a faster time than Brian, something funny happened to me. For some reason, I began to think that I really was a better-than-average runner, capable of running distances much farther than 3.1 miles without puking.

Maybe it was delusions of athletic grandeur caused by my friend's shocking disbelief in my ability to finish a 5K with relative ease. Maybe it was a chemical imbalance from drinking gallons of water mixed with Mountain Blast Powerade during a summer spent training. Maybe it was the false confidence that came whenever I blared 2Pac and Dr. Dre's "California Love" through my iPod Nano while racing through an imagined gang-ridden and gritty South Central Los Angeles neighborhood. Whatever it was, shortly after that race I convinced myself I could tackle the mother of all races: a marathon. And the more I thought about it, the more it made sense. I had grown increasingly tired of hearing about people like me of marginal fitness levels who had run marathons. "Why can't I?" I thought. Things were clicking for me, especially my previously unreliable body. My notoriously weak back felt strong somehow. My recurrent tendonitis hadn't flared up again. And most importantly, I remained in complete control over my sphincter muscle, even during my twenty-mile training runs.

So after months of uncharacteristic discipline—made possible with a somewhat condescending but generally helpful training guide, *Marathon: You Can Do It!*—and with the blessing of an especially supportive wife, the big day finally arrived. It was the morning of the Twin Cities Marathon, and I was finally ready to compete—like a real adult.

I CAN; I WILL

My marathon morning ritual began like all the other grueling mornings of my long runs. I was up before dawn quietly moaning in the dimmed light of my bathroom, taping my toes and covering my nipples with two oversized Band-Aids to prevent chafing and bleeding. (Sounds funny, but the alternative is no laughing matter, trust me.)

This morning, however, there was one notable exception to my routine. Months prior, I had heard that marathoners like to personalize their shirts, arms, or legs by inscribing their names or funny motivational phrases on them. This way, the cheering crowd could more intimately connect with the runners, encouraging them by name. Always the music fan, it didn't take me long to decide that I wanted to run with the Prince logo on my shirt. But after weeks of burning holes through thin layers of my patented "moisture-wicking" performance shirts trying to iron on a makeshift decal, it was time to grab a Sharpie and be done with it. And since I can barely draw a stick figure, let alone that glyph icon, I opted for simply writing a motivational mantra. In block letters, I scribbled "I CAN" down my left arm and "I WILL" down my right.

Staring at myself in the mirror, I flexed my muscles. I felt like a warrior painted for battle . . . . An Ancient Greek preparing to run from Marathon to Athens to announce victory over the Persians . . . . An athlete! Finally! And then I realized something. When my arms moved up and down, and the skin flexed and folded on my biceps, my temporary tattoos weren't really all that legible. My confidence dropped a bit as I imagined myself lumbering through the racecourse with the crowd on my left shouting, "Keep it up, Ian!" while the mob on the right yelled, "Looking good, Will!"

No matter, I thought. Nothing's getting in my way today, I told myself. I have only two goals: finish the race and don't soil myself. I can. I will.

For one day, I would run farther than I had ever run before.

MARATHON MAN GUY

Finding a place in the starting chute for the four-hour pace group, I committed to racing alongside a collection of runners who presumably would walk a little, laugh a little, and enjoy the challenge a lot. I had confidence in my ability to keep that pace and that my smart-ass inner monologue would keep me company.

MILE MARKER 1

What a scene! Roads clogged with happy runners. And check out all these supporters . . . every inch of the curb, cheering us on. This is like some kind of movie. And Colin, you're the star! Keep it in check though. Pace yourself. Leave something for the finish. Hey, you know what? Maybe you really can do this in four hours! Yes. Four hours is yours . . . I can! I will!

MILE MARKER 3

These fans are crazy loud! So cool! I'm gonna come out here next year and join them. Those cowbells are everywhere. What did that runner up there say? More cowbell? Oh yeah! That SNL *skit! Funny stuff! Sure helps to laugh. Stay loose. Not serious.*

MILE MARKER 6

Hey, is that a guy I work with running next to me? "Jon? Yeah, it's me, Colin! I didn't know you were running this, too." *I've always liked him.* "Is this your first marathon, too? What? Your ninth?" *Prick.* "Hey, that's great. A little crazy, but great. I'll call you tomorrow. See how you did. Good luck!" *Maybe I'm running too fast. I'm passing him, and he's done eight of these before. I'll bet he knows something that I don't know.*

MILE MARKER 11

Okay, let's find a Porta-Potty. Pronto. Wait. . . . No, you don't need one. You're fine. What's that? More cowbell, somebody said? Is that the same joker up there? Nope, different runner, same joke. I guess we runners are all on the same wavelength. Okay, you do need to go to the bathroom. Where did this come from? You've never had to stop a run before! That's fine, that's fine. Lots of people stop, I guess. Okay, Okay, here's a short line for the Porta-Potty. Let's take care of business.

MILE MARKER 12

Whew! Feeling good. Much lighter. Lovin' it. So what if you just lost eleven minutes waiting in line to use a toilet? You did the right thing by ignoring your accidental adult instincts and not dropping trou in the woods like you considered at mile 10. Yes. Four hours. Four hours. I can still make that.

MILE MARKER 18

Okay, this is starting to suck now. Big time. But just two miles to go, and it's the twenty-mile marker that everyone talks about. The real race just begins at mile twenty they say. Assholes. Everyone with running shoes is an expert. I won't hit the wall. I've done twenty miles three times before. What's another six?

MILE MARKER 21

Goddamn hill. It's going to destroy my four hours. But you're not walking it like these other pansies. You've been here before. You can take it. Okay, that's the ninth time I've heard the "more cowbell" joke. People, it's not funny anymore. Ugh. Feeling like Batman from the TV show: Losing strength . . . can't breathe . . . must . . . fight . . .this . . . somehow . . . .

MILE MARKER 22

Screw that four-hour bullshit! Who the hell do you think you are? Just finish this son-of-a-bitch! Just finish. When is this hill going to end? And could a few hundred of you fans please go away?

Don't you have homes? Your condescending "You can do it guys!" cheering isn't helping me keep my cookies down. You're just clogging up the curbs waiting for me to puke aren't you? Okay, think positively. Think positively. If you keel over now, you can rest for twenty minutes and walk the rest. So technically, you've already won. Yeah, you're a winner. That's it. One leg in front of the other.

MILE MARKER 23

God, it hurts, it hurts, it hurts! Keep at it though. Breathing is decent. Bowels are fine. Legs are shot, but your arms can pull you. Hey! It's Kelly and the kids! "Yeah, it's Daddy! Hi guys! Love you! Thank you! Daddy's gonna make it!" *Daddy's gonna puke. In spectacular fashion. I'll make the front page. No, no, no, I'm gonna make it. Gonna make it.*

MILE MARKER 24

I'm drinking tonight. A lot of beer. Don't walk. Keep running. I can. I will.

MILE MARKER 25

Beer. Cold, cold beer. I'm swimming in a pool of icy cold beer, gulping it down. So refreshing. Who's that approaching me? Pamela Anderson from Baywatch? *She just jumped into my beer pool! And now she's slow-motion water running in my direction to pull me toward the finish line. Come to me, CJ! You can pull me! SNAP OUT OF IT, LOSER! You've got one mile to go! Don't drift off just yet!*

MILE MARKER 26

I don't believe it! There's the finish line race clock up ahead. How am I doing? . . . four hours, twenty-seven minutes and counting. Shit! Ah, who cares? You're a minute from finishing, and your pants are dry. Not everyone can say that. Eyes are tearing up. Try not to cry. They've got a camera that takes your picture about here. Annnnnnd . . . done! Gimme that medal! Beer tonight. A lot of beer.

JUST DUPE IT

OK, you might be thinking, "So he ran a marathon. BFD!" Well, it is a big deal. Why? Because much like my surprise at becoming someone who can't stay up past midnight anymore, I never imagined in my wildest dreams that someday I would care so much about competing in such an athletic activity—especially an event that occasionally offers its participants a moderate level of athletic acceptance among real adults who tend to keep score.

So if I can do it, you probably can, too. How? Well, clearly a caustic monologue can help encourage you through a test of endurance. But there's more. My jogging journeys have taught me a few newfound tricks that any reluctant grownup can apply whenever a situation sucks you unwittingly into life's overly serious athletic arenas. In fact, with a little bit of help, I've found that any accidental adult of modest athletic prowess can fake his way through the wider world of athletics, not just marathon running. All it takes is some quick thinking, a little creativity, and some occasional trickery.

Inspired by my Herculean effort and my training guide, *Marathon: You Can Do It!*, I'd like to offer you my own fitness manual for mastering the manly domain of sports.

ATHLETICS: YOU CAN DO THEM!

AVOID COMPETITION AT ALL COSTS

Want to shoot hoops? *Sure!* Play a little one-on-one? *No thanks!*
Care to throw the baseball? *Sounds like fun!* Play a game? *Sounds like trouble!*

Who wants to hit the tennis ball? *I do!* Who wants to play some doubles matches? *I don't!*

As soon as someone starts to keep score, your athletic inadequacies can now become quantified. How much fun is that? And instead of ending the activity feeling good about getting a little exercise, tallied points ensure that now there's going to be a defined winner and a defined loser at the end. Makes you want to say, "Lighten up, Francis! It's only a game!" Yet some testosterone-bursting adults cannot lighten up, and many might not take no for an answer. So if athletic contests prove impossible to avoid, choose the ones that only offer individual, mano-a-mano competition, and never join team sports. This way when you lose, the only one you can blame is yourself. And since you love yourself, there's no guilt, no remorse, no apologies necessary to teammates, and no lingering hard feelings!

TRY A DIFFERENT KIND OF NOONER

Want to maximize the attention you receive for exercising? Do it during a lunch break from the office. Going to the club to lift weights or run on the treadmill for a while will boost more than your afternoon productivity. It elevates your status with coworkers who see your grit, your dedication, your heart. And if for some reason they didn't witness your high-profile midday departure to the parking lot with your gym bag slung over your shoulder, then consider a high-profile running route along nearby congested highways or densely populated parks and trails. Then create a plausible (but ultimately unnecessary) excuse to invite your colleagues into your office when you return, so they can see you freshly showered and eating your lunch at your desk. If you're lucky, a curious coworker might throw you a gift by asking why your hair is wet. Be careful to inform her of your cardiovascular regimen without coming off like a pretentious douchebag (if that's possible).

WEAR IT WELL

Want to fool others into believing you are super sports-minded and possibly even more athletically active than you actually are? Try sports apparel. From baseball caps to football jerseys, your athletically suggestive weekend wardrobe says, "I not only support this team, but I may even possess the skills necessary to join the team." But before you throw on your Tar Heel blue, be prepared to discuss the team. Can you name the coach or a few players? Know their record this year? If you can't share it, then don't wear it. Because for many adults, even casual athletic gear is considered an open conversation starter. That's why I typically wear shirts, sweatshirts, and caps that simply say "IRISH." If I'm lucky, the casual observer might think I'm a fan. And at worst, if anyone should want to talk a little Notre Dame football, I can quickly renounce any perceived allegiance or familiarity with the team and simply offer the truthful explanation, "Sorry, man. I'm wearing this for my ancestors, not for the team." This pretense may still offend a true fan, but in the world of sports apparel transgressions it's a far weaker affront than the crime of those rubes who feel the need to customize a professional sports jersey with their own name. If you're going to be that guy—and I pray that you won't—then at least have the common decency to use the generic number 00 instead of your sports hero's number. Because wearing a Chicago Bulls number 23 jersey that says "Whipperdale" or "Goldfarb" isn't clever or funny; it's just stupid and wrong.

DISAPPEAR YOUR GEAR

If you were paying attention to my advice in Chapter 8, you've learned the value of blaming your unhandiness on faulty tools or the altogether absence of the necessary tools to complete a repair project. The same principles apply to athletics. Your entire set of $30 golf clubs can't possibly be expected to perform as proficiently as your neighbor's $300 driver; therefore, why even try? Likewise, if you don't own a pair of ice skates, you can't quite play a pickup game of pond hockey, can you? If a super jock is extraordinarily persistent in attempting to draft your participation, remember that claiming to have unusual body dimensions may be necessary in order to convincingly rebuff offers of loaned sports equipment.

ALWAYS CHOOSE THE SHIRTS TEAM

Still have that thirty-inch waist from college? And how's your metabolism these days? Thought so. When teams divide up and start to choose which side is shirts and which is skins, please, please, choose wisely. Women and children may be watching.

FAKE AN INJURY

Good actor? If so, sports offer the perfect stage to demonstrate a flair for the dramatic. When you're faced with unwanted competition, you can always fake your way out of it. Depending on your acting ability, choose from the following degrees of deception.

Dinner Theater Thespians

Few people have the energy to second-guess claims of persistent, recurring injuries that flare up at inopportune times (like most every time you play a sport). So put your acting chops to the test. Didn't grab that rebound? Grab your knee instead, fall to the court, and explain to your teammates how bursitis has affected your lift. Missed returning that serve in racquetball? Ouch! There's that old ACL injury again. That partial tear never really healed properly after high school. For those even less-creative actors, remember that muscle cramps, sprained ankles, and tendonitis are universally accepted standbys and fairly easy to fake.

Academy Award Winners

Want to earn some serious adult sports cred without really doing too much to deserve it? Step in front of a charging point guard. Lean into a softball fast pitch. Run into a speeding cornerback. For maximum effect and reward, simply position yourself to get slightly injured, in stunning fashion, very early into the game. Sure, it might not take much acting to convince others of your excruciating pain. But when the oxygen returns to your lungs, and the stars behind your eyes extinguish, you can hobble over to the sidelines and remain there the rest of the season, having earned some respect for taking a hit and getting back up.

HEAVY MEDAL

On the ride home from my glorious marathon triumph, I must have been deliriously exhausted because I remember letting my kids take turns wearing my finisher's medal. And that's the last time I've let those greasy little fingers toy with my priceless treasure. Today it hangs around a framed photo of me taken a few miles after my liberating bathroom break. I'm smiling, of course.

It makes perfect sense that I should cherish that medal. As Kelly correctly points out regularly, I often think I deserve an award for most tasks I accomplish whether they're stellar achievements or simply folding the laundry once a month. So after running for four and a half hours in one shot? Damn straight I deserve a medal!

Because of that blue-ribboned silver disk, my son Finnegan now thinks I won the race. And who am I to argue? I suppose I could teach him a lesson that winning doesn't really matter, but I imagine he's already picked that up from me. Nope, I'll milk the medal for all it's worth. In fact, that night, after indeed drinking a lot of beer, I warned Kelly that I someday plan to wear the medal out to a party or to a school board meeting . . . or worse . . . that I'll wear it around my bare chest sitting upright in bed some hot summer night giving her my best "Yeah, Baby!" look.

Truth be told, now that I've finally sampled a taste of athletic accomplishment, I can see how performing well in a sport can become intoxicating for the average adult male. Sure, my membership in the Adult Athletic Club is precarious at best. But at least now I have an out when sports conversations come up. Like the guy who finally breaks par or pulls a freak hole-in-one out of his ass, I plan to play the "I ran a marathon" card anytime I feel the need to assimilate into the adult world of sports talk, if for no other reason than to temporarily shut up those arrogant adult jock blowhards who can't let high school go.

I'm in no position to suggest what particular athletic accomplishment you should pursue, but if you can find a sport or activity you don't completely suck at, then nurture it and hang onto it for dear life. Because in the game of life, excelling at an adult athletic activity feels like winning—and accidental adults like us need to take our victories where we can find them, no matter how small. Any time we can stick together and put forth a total team effort against our assimilated adult opponents, maybe, just maybe, our accomplishments can silence the crowd.

f us never planned o
his happening. But it di
ometime between gra
chool and our first mort
age, a strange phenom
non began replacing ou
outhful mojos with
ew-found maturity. An
e didn't see it coming
ur two-door coupe
orphed into sliding
or minivans. Bar-hop
ng turned into movi
ghts on the couch. Now
e write letters to th
itor. And golfo. It'o n

11. HOBBIES

"Adult" Entertainment (Not *That* Kind!)

HIGH SCHOOL REUNIONS ARE great measuring sticks for adulthood. In the time it takes you to work the high school gymnasium nursing a gin and tonic (nice forced adult drink choice!), most of us can determine how far our formerly fun classmates have progressed in their inevitable assimilation to the adult world. Unfortunately, our friends also discover where we accidental adults stand in comparison.

> "What do you do with your free time?"
>
> —David Letterman

> "I'm just doin' karate and tryin' to get females pregnant."
>
> —Tracy Morgan

Female classmate: "Did I tell you I'm about to make partner at the law firm?"

Outward response: "I always knew you'd be successful."

Inner monologue: *I never knew you'd be this attractive!*

At my reunion, it didn't take me long to learn exactly what my childhood friends thought of my post–high school progression. After hearing them tell me, "My God! You haven't changed a bit!" no fewer than a dozen times, I quickly realized my classmates were giving me their unofficial award for "The Least Changed." Given the choice, I decided to take their assessment as a compliment of aging gracefully rather than a potential indictment of immaturity, and I proceeded to spend the rest of the night guzzling light beer and reliving the glory days of my youth.

The next morning as I drove through the winding county highways of rural Wisconsin on my three-hour journey back to the St. Paul suburbs, I started flipping through the "Where Are They Now?" program our reunion organizers had assembled. I browsed my classmates' bios, catching up on their family lives, their occupations, and their most pride-inspiring accomplishments. In my own biography I had revealed my zeal for writing, running, and drumming. But as I began to scan over each alum's "Hobbies and Interests" section, I knew what was coming before I read even one word. Yes, as varied and diverse as our class had become, most of my classmates would share a set of universal interests supported by unmistakable skills that I do not possess. And I was right. Using loathsome and vile verbs like *camping, ice fishing, hunting, canoeing, hiking,* and *snowmobiling,* damn near every one of my classmates perfectly illustrated the Continental Divide separating us.

When it comes to favorite pastime activities, those Cheeseheads thrive in the outdoors. This former Cheesehead? Not so much.

PLAYIN' 5 TO 9

I firmly believe that what makes each of us truly unique among our peers is not what we do between 9 A.M. and 5 P.M. but how we occupy our time between 5 P.M. and 9 A.M. Don't believe me? Try this icebreaker at your next cocktail party. Ask someone you've never met before what she does for a living and try, really try, to appear captivated instead of bored to tears. Then approach a completely different stranger and ask her what hobby really lights her fire (when she's not working her mind-numbing, thankless job). Unless that first guest is a dolphin trainer, a stuntwoman, or an aerobics instructor, I guarantee you'll find the second stranger infinitely more fascinating. And probably better looking.

So if it's true that your job reveals you're just another fool who has been jobbed, but it's your interests that makes you interesting, then you'll want to secure a hobby or two that sounds impressive to others. An added bonus is if you actually enjoy said hobby. Trouble is, for many accidental adults, the most common and typical adult recreations are of little value or interest.

- While real adults are out hiking the trails, you'd prefer to enjoy nature as depicted through a 1080p high-definition PBS documentary in the comforts of a climate-controlled sun room.
- When the neighborhood men want to deal you into a quick hand of poker, you'd rather forgo the formality of the game, avoid the certain humiliation, and simply offer them your wallet.
- Late-night fun for many assimilated adults involves a favorite board game like Trivial Pursuit, Monopoly, or Clue. But you'd rather load up an iPod party mix, hit "shuffle," play the first two seconds of each song, and award points for the first person to name that '80s tune.

Unfortunately, when most adults discuss their hobbies, the conversation quickly moves into a recruitment effort, and they're often less than truthful. Passion obscures logic. Potential dangers are sugarcoated. Costs are hidden. Boredom becomes sold as excitement. So before you commit to taking on a new pastime or two, it's important to know what you can expect. You need the skinny on some of the most common hobbies and interests embraced by intentional adults.

Lucky for you, I still abide by the Boy Scouts' motto, Be Prepared, and I can offer you:

THE UNNATURALISTS' FIELD GUIDE TO THE OUTDOORS AND OTHER RIDICULOUS ADULT RECREATIONS

THE OUTDOORS

Let's begin with the most common and least interesting recreational activity known to assimilated man: enjoying the outdoors. You might think that growing up amid Midwestern fields, marshes, and forests would have instilled in me an intimate understanding of the outdoors and the ability to proficiently navigate nature's offerings. It didn't. In fact, my years spent observing outdoors enthusiasts have raised more questions than answers, questions that tend to infuriate true naturalists, such as:

- Can any reasonable couple actually consider an outward bound weekend a romantic getaway when the itinerary includes tramping across dusty trails, bathing in leech-filled ponds, and defecating behind trees?
- Why would reasonable parents give their kids a few dirty tree branches, a pocketknife, and a bag of marshmallows and

send them off to an unsupervised campfire where the shoving matches inevitably begin?

- Why do so many anglers avidly advocate properly releasing a fish back to the water (*Gently push and pull the fish through the water to aerate its gills . . . .*) after you just enticed it to swallow a barbed hook?
- Why does something as simple as the pure, uncorrupted experience of walking up a hill require hundreds of dollars of sophisticated hiking equipment and navigational gear?
- How can you *not* laugh when someone suggests pitching a tent? ("I see someone already has" is my stock response.)

Of course, my disinterest and ineptitude in many outdoors activities makes me something of an anomaly among my more adept, nature-loving peers. But when it comes to the world of accidental adults, I'm right at home. Once again, we reluctant grownups realize that true adults embrace outdoors activities with confidence primarily because they know what they're doing. The accidental adults? Well . . . I'll bet you know what I'm talking about:

- Sure, you've probably upgraded your fishing rod and reel from your three-foot yellow and white Snoopy fishing pole with the push-button line release. But you and your shiny new spin-cast reel still might generate snickers when you go jigging for walleyes with a bobber still attached to your line.
- If push comes to shove, you could probably build a neat little charcoal pyramid inside a mini Weber grill. But who's got an hour to sit around and wait patiently while the charcoals turn a light gray indicating they're finally burning evenly? So after your seventh generous application of Zippo, whose fault is it

that the bright pink center of your burgers tastes like lighter fluid? That's right. The tree-hugging purist who insists your camping trip is illegitimate if you cook with propane.

- Of course you know how to properly cut branches off a tree and chop them up for future camp firewood. All it took was a stunned but merciful neighbor who insisted you borrow his bow saw (a remarkable device that's seemingly designed for cross-cutting branches) after he watched you take a handsaw to your silver maple's limbs.

Before you commit to a weekend in the wilderness or a boondoggle in the boondocks, be sure you understand what you're up against in pursuing this recreational activity.

MATERIALS NEEDED

You might think choosing an outdoors hobby would require an endless supply list. Not necessarily. There's only one purchase that's absolutely critical, and it may even become your only acquisition: an outdoor thermometer. If this life-saving device ever points to a number lower than 60°F, the outing is cancelled, and you will never need to procure any other gear.

NECESSARY SKILLS

The ability to anticipate how an invitation to the "Weekend Up North" evolves into the inevitable "*Weak*end Up North."

The Invitation

"Looks like another beautiful weekend forecast. Why don't you and the family come up to our lake home?"

The Inevitable

"Welcome to our cabin! Watch your step kids. We'll get that rotted-out deckboard nailed back down sooner or later. Come to think of it, maybe you all can help with that this weekend! It's kind of our family cabin tradition. We spend 95 percent of our waking moments performing backbreaking repairs and maintenance up here. Relaxation? That's for the six-hour car ride home, silly!

"What's that smell, you ask? Beats me. We hardly smell anything in here anymore. Mothballs and damp asbestos, you'd guess? Well, I was going to say it could be decaying field mice that occasionally get trapped and die in our walls, but sure, anything's possible.

"Bet you could use a cold one! Hey, not so fast, wise guy! Let's put Mr. Budweiser back in our icebox until the kids go to bed. Not to worry, though. Our well water tastes incredible—now that the township wrapped up its final radon analysis. What's that? You'd prefer bottled water? This ain't the Ritz my friend! Oh, that reminds me, you may have noticed we finally have indoor plumbing. We're even thinking about getting a water heater in a few years, too. So go ahead and enjoy an invigorating shower in the morning. I'll bet it's a quick one!

"Let me show you to your room. Up, up, up you go! Doesn't climbing a splintering indoor ladder just take you back to child-hood? There's nothing like sleeping in a loft, I say, no matter your age!

"Ouch! Careful not to bump your head on those rafters! What, is this your first time maneuvering around a four-foot-tall bedroom? Just remember, if you and the Mrs. are feeling frisky tonight, forget about it! The rest of us will be right below you in the living room shaking Yahtzee dice 'til the wee hours of the

morning. *Anything to fend off the crushing boredom of sharing this confined space with friends and family every weekend for three months.*

"Well, enough of the tour. Let's head outside to the lake. You'll love our beach. The water's so clear you can see three feet down right to the roots of the milfoil weeds that have infested our landing. The kids say swimming here feels like walking through an evergreen forest naked, but I tell them the weeds are a blessing. Our family of snapping turtles just loves them. Do they bite? Don't tell me you've never been bitten by a turtle before! It's more like a stinging nip, really. Next thing you'll tell me you'll want to use salt to remove the leeches from your legs. Hell, me and the kids just tug 'em right off. Toughen up! We're in their world now!

"Hey! Now, where did those clouds move in from? Rain wasn't in my forecast! Oh well. We can outlast these torrential downpours. Back indoors for some more fun! Have I shown you our adorable six-inch black-and-white TV?"

TIME REQUIRED

The pursuit of pleasure in the not-so-great outdoors can suck up quite a bit of time. In fact, during the summer months many of my friends and neighbors will literally disappear around 4 P.M. every Friday only to return from God knows where around 6 P.M. on Sunday. As a result, the short attention span of the typical accidental adult needs to be considered before committing to an endless weekend journey into the elements.

Should you still find yourself along for the ride, what's the best way to pass the time? Townie bars.

BEFORE BEGINNING, ASK YOURSELF . . .

Can I convince others that I'm an experienced outdoorsman without having to prove it? Success requires a series of well-constructed excuses at the ready. Here are a few that have served me well over the years:

Camping trip? Nah. You wouldn't want to share a tent with me. I'm a sleepwalker with a weak bladder and poor aim.

Hunting? Yeah, I know a thing or two about guns. When I was eight I fired a .22 at Boy Scouts camp. Seems just like yesterday that the Scoutmaster took away my Fire Arms Safety merit badge. Sure, I can join you, but my wife insists I wear full body armor. That's probably a good idea for you, too.

Fishing trip? I've heard the fish don't start biting 'til around noon, which is about the time I like to wake up when I'm on vacation. Does that work for you? If so, I'll go as long as there is no Charlie Daniels Band, .38 Special, Garth Brooks, or Neil Young on the roadtrip up. (Note: This very reasonable soundtrack request is an effective and universal deal killer for any road trip, no matter the destination. Apply as needed.)

Hiking in the bluffs? Where's the nearest wireless tower?

DON'T BE SURPRISED IF . . .

Your friends eventually conclude you don't care for the outdoors, and their invitations cease. Well done!

BE SURE TO TELL PEOPLE . . .

Nature is God's masterpiece. But a roof, four walls, a picture window, and a thermostat are pretty damn beautiful, too.

HOME BREWING

The older I get, the more easily annoyed I've become by the tired, ridiculous, and just plain stupid shit that adults sometimes say. Sure, there are some universally despised expressions, such as "At the end of the day . . ." or "It is what it is." But we all have different and uniquely sensitive triggers to language that send us hurdling over the edge. Lately, I've decided the most annoying six-word string in the world is, "You've got to read my blog!" A very close second would be, "You've got to try my homebrew!"

Beware of any hobby that accidental adults first nurtured in college and that real adults dabble in today. Granted, there was a time when mixing up a batch of homebrew in your dorm room closet was daring, exciting, and worthy of BMOC status. But that was back when you were underage, perpetually broke, and looking for a challenge to outsmart those lame-ass nosy hall directors. So what's the point now?

I know many guys will say they genuinely love the craft of home brewing. They consider it an art form of sorts . . . a labor of love. I'd be more easily convinced of the merits of their endeavor if it ever produced something truly lovable, much less drinkable. It rarely does. I've tried a lot of lagers in my life, including dozens of homemade beers pushed on me by friends, and not a single one was worth trying again. In fact, most tasted like a glass of room-temperature, day-old coffee with a surprising yet disturbing hint of cough syrup in the aftertaste. So why do they bother? Here's why I won't.

MATERIALS NEEDED

The inexplicable popularity of this hobby has sparked an industry that produces some very comprehensive and easy-to-acquire beginner's brew kits and sets of ingredients. The costs of home brewing kits aren't prohibitive, but the choices are. Which recipe do you want to try first? An English brown ale? Perhaps a German pilsner? How about an amber hybrid beer, or even a classic doppelbock? I've heard the ladies like a fun spiced-herb beer, but shouldn't you offer them a sour ale first? By the time you sort out all the choices and finally pick your poison, you could've downed a six of Sam Adams already.

Another challenge to consider is where you are going to store your fermenting buckets of liquid fun. Of course, if you're married, this decision is likely not yours to make, which means you can expect your recreational choice will be relegated to the basement crawlspace. Quite the endorsement of a worthwhile hobby.

NECESSARY SKILLS

Brewing your own beer? It's not rocket science! (Sorry to those whose trigger I just flipped with that annoying phrase. For a fuller apology, "You've got to read my blog!") But it's true. In the world of hobbies, home brewing ranks as more challenging than stamp-collecting, but it's a tad less complicated than mastering the martial arts. What it does require is time. And there's the rub.

TIME REQUIRED

If you're as impatient as I am, remember that the home-brewing process includes proper brew time, the fermentation process, bottling and labeling your beer, and bottle conditioning, which allows beer to carbonate. Add it all up, and you're looking at about a solid month before you can actually enjoy your product. Compare this to a ten-minute roundtrip beer run to your local liquor store, and your choice is crystal clear.

BEFORE BEGINNING, ASK YOURSELF . . .

Do you really want to drink anything concocted in a five-gallon bucket?

DON'T BE SURPRISED IF . . .

Your beer tastes like chilled squirrel urine.

BE SURE TO TELL PEOPLE . . .

"You've got to try my homemade beer! It does not taste like chilled squirrel urine."

COACHING YOUTH ATHLETICS

If I've mastered any lesson during my reluctant journey into accidental adulthood, it would be the mantra "Play to your strengths." Your sanity, and ultimately your survival, depends on it.

As you know by now, my strengths are essentially limited to a handful of marginal talents and even fewer interests. So I suppose this is why I've chosen to spend a good chunk of my free time producing an annual nightclub-style music show for my church. Now I know what you're thinking. Church + music = lame entertainment. On the contrary, this event features some really topnotch, homegrown talent performing an eclectic mix of pop, rock, swing, blues, and folk songs—none of which metaphorically asks Jesus to take the wheel or melodramatically proclaims "I've been redeemed!" (And we serve alcohol, which always helps elevate the vibe of our sold-out shows.)

I also subscribe to the theory that successfully playing to your strengths also requires avoiding your weaknesses. And for me, there's a long list of activities to avoid, chief among them being anything that combines competitive athletics and mentoring other people's children. So it's little surprise that year after year I strategically escape the clutches of one of the most common volunteer traps known to man—the youth athletics coach.

Believe me when I say that, for the right person, this hobby can be a satisfyingly selfless gift of time to offer community youth. But for me, it's just not suited to my skills quite like producing a nightclub show. And so I say, to each his own.

- While I'm spending a weekend at auditions to cast the show, volunteer football coaches are holding their combine-style tryouts. (If I had to field a team, I'd put the beefy kids on the line and the skinny kids in the backfield. Does it require more talent evaluation than that?)
- While I'm helping my bandmates figure out the best key in which to play "Don't Stop Believin'," volunteer basketball coaches are running pick-and-roll drills from the top of the key. (If pressed, I couldn't tell you which is the pick and which is the roll. Pretty sure I know where the key is, though.)
- While I'm worrying that we didn't buy enough wine for the shows, little league coaches are coordinating whose turn it is to bring the postgame juice boxes and snacks. (I'd obliviously end up serving Nutter Butters to the peanut-allergy kids.)

I realize that volunterring to produce a music program and coaching a Little Dribbler's basketball team aren't mutually exclusive activities. But for now, I'm going to keep playing to my strengths, avoid life's unnecessarily competitive situations, and let the intentional adults play coach to my kids. If you're like me, you might consider following this path as well.

MATERIALS NEEDED

- **Playbooks and rulebooks:** Both are considered must reads, especially for an accidental adult who's decided on coaching. For example, in a beginner's football playbook, the offense is usually depicted as Os and the defense as Xs. Telling your team that an easy way to remember the difference is by thinking of Os as hugs and Xs as kisses won't resonate very well, unless your players are already receiving sugary-sweet text messages from fourth-grade girls. XOXOXO! Likewise, a well-written basketball rulebook will explain that when the referee blows the whistle, stops the game, and signals a letter *T* in your direction, after you've simply offered him your glasses, he's not granting you a time-out. (Well, in a way . . .)
- **Uniforms:** At some levels of youth competition, some adult coaches have been known to don an adult-sized version of their team's uniform. Trouble is, many of these uniforms appear to be exact replicas, right down to the youth medium size. Better run a few more laps with the team before squeezing into that costume.
- **A multipassenger vehicle:** Invariably (and unfortunately) you'll need as many available seats in your vehicle as possible at the

end of nearly every practice when an absent-minded accidental adult parent fails to pick up his kid on time.

NECESSARY SKILLS

- **Patience:** I really admire volunteer coaches, yet I hold no illusions of ever learning from their examples. Nearly every successful coach I've ever met has been gifted with a patience gene not found in my genetic code. Good for them. Not so good for me. (Or for my kids.)
- **Restraint:** When you coach children, you're going to see a lot of goofy and sloppy behavior. Adult conduct, however, requires you to call juvenile players by their real names and not by the more colorful and accurate descriptors that naturally pop into your head, like Flopper Boy or Concussion Kid or Freeballer or Mr. Stumbles.

TIME REQUIRED

Nearly every Saturday morning of your life, robbing you of precious REM time. This alone is a deal killer for many chronically fatigued accidental adults like me for whom rest is golden and sleep is sacred.

BEFORE BEGINNING, ASK YOURSELF . . .

If I can barely concentrate long enough to finish a driveway game of H-O-R-S-E with my son, how can I legitimately ask twelve hyperactive boys to keep their heads in the game for thirty consecutive minutes?

DON'T BE SURPRISED IF . . .

Your kids' coaches ask you to help assistant-coach a game or two. Such is the level of desperation at this level of athletics.

BE SURE TO TELL PEOPLE . . .

"You know that trick play where the first baseman pretended to throw the ball to the pitcher and then tagged out the runner as he led off toward second base? That was my call, not coach's." (If the umpire rules that stunt unfair at the Little League level, it was the coach's decision—and so bush league.)

HOME THEATERS

By now we've all learned that life isn't fair, for many reasons. Chief among them is the fact that you can't always pick your neighbors. But what if you could pick their occupations? Who would you want living next door? For the accidental adult, this hypothetical is a no-brainer. You'd want to share the cul-de-sac with an electrician, a computer networker, and a home theater installation specialist. It would seem, then, a stroke of good luck that my brother Ryan fits this description almost perfectly, with one small exception. The bastard lives 1,600 miles away from my needs. As a result, I have to troubleshoot every electrical, computer, or A/V complication I experience long-distance. And for me, it gets complicated pretty fast.

Like many older brothers, Ryan is routinely shocked and disgusted by my lack of mechanical skill. As a way of coping with his scorn, I've decided his disappointment in me has more to do with him than me. I easily arrived at this conclusion by looking no further than at his most recent accomplishment—his self-built home theater featuring a 100-foot front-projection screen framed by motorized black velvet curtains, a 7.1 surround-sound system, two rows of stadium-seating-mounted home theater chairs, a full HD-resolution projector mounted in a custom hush-box at the rear, and a shitload of Monster speaker cabling (THX-certified of course). Aside from George Lucas himself, I'm not sure what his screening room is missing.

Yes, by all accounts, my brother is an electronics snob. You know the type. Within two seconds of a film's opening credit sequence, he can detect an inferiorly wired surround-sound system. With just a glance, he can pick the one 720i resolution monitor out of a lineup of 1080p LCD television sets on a showroom floor. And like any home theater purist, he can tell you why a surge protector is way more necessary than a power conditioner. (Huh?) Guys like him straddle a fine line between justified pride and annoying arrogance. And the phrase "That quality is good enough" has never been a part of their vocabulary. But the truth is, many accidental adults envy these guys. Myself included. Who among us accidental adults wouldn't want the technical skills and knowledge commonly associated with home theater enthusiasts? So why not pursue this hobby that quickly becomes a passion?

MATERIALS NEEDED

Money. And lots of it.

NECESSARY SKILLS

- The ability to drill holes and snake cabling and wires through walls, ceilings, and floors of multiple levels of your home leaving virtually no visible evidence of wiring. (If you can do this, generations should sing your praises in folksongs. I know I will.)

- The ability to correctly map and label all those wires to input/ output jacks of the TV, TiVo DVR, receiver, Wii, and DVD player so you're not SOL when your six-year-old disconnects that tangled mess of cables while digging behind the entertainment center looking for her *Dora the Explorer* bingo game DVD.

- The ability to effectively achieve complete noise isolation. Remember, sound proofing is not so much to keep your room's volume from spilling over into other areas of the home but to prevent the clamor of your wife's verbal harassment and untimely requests for your assistance from spoiling your fun.

TIME REQUIRED

When considering the time involved in properly cultivating a home theater hobby, you really need to break it down into four principal areas: research, installation, maintenance, and enjoyment. If you're like me, you will spend months plunging head-first and wide-eyed into the initial phase of research—reading online electronics articles, measuring proper viewing distances, searching for the most affordable equipment—only to be discouraged the moment you realize the seventeen-year-old kid at the big box electronics chain store knows more about the audio/visual universe than you've ever learned about your own remote control. The next kicker comes during the weekend-long installation phase when you discover (midproject) that you're in over your head, and unless your brother answers his cell phone right-the-hell-now, your kids' impending slumber party/ movie night won't include that little "movie" part of the festivities.

Mercifully, the maintenance phase of a home theater hobby requires the least amount of your time simply because (like most accidental adults' home improvement projects) you won't properly upkeep or support your equipment, despite your best intentions to always remain current. Finally comes the enjoyment time, the amount of which is entirely dependant upon others with whom you share a house and ultimately proves far less than you had ever imagined.

BEFORE BEGINNING, ASK YOURSELF . . .

Can my marriage or long-term relationship withstand the absences associated with home theater research, installation, maintenance, and enjoyment?

DON'T BE SURPRISED IF . . .

Your marriage or long-term relationship cannot withstand the absences associated with home theater research, installation, maintenance, and enjoyment.

BE SURE TO TELL PEOPLE . . .

"Yes, I installed this home theater by myself" (justifying your own private definition of the word *myself* as meaning your brother, your buddy, and the entire customer service team at Stressed Buy).

RECREATION RECOMMENDATION

In classic accidental adult fashion, I've spent several pages summarily dismissing a series of activities as unworthy of a reluctant grownup's time. So what hobbies would I recommend? Picking a pastime is such a personal choice, about all I can suggest is the one activity I'd embrace if I had more time, more money, and more consideration of others (longshots, I know).

COOKING

I'm perfectly happy spending my free time reading, writing, running, playing the drums, or enjoying quality time with my family. (Did that last one sound too forced?) Yet if I were ever pressed to find another pastime, cooking would top a very short list. The benefits of knowing your way around the kitchen are considerable, especially for a guy. Why?

Men in general aren't expected to know much about preparing an exquisite meal. As a result, they rarely try. In fact, I know plenty of accidental adults who simply eat cereal for dinner many nights, with no complaints. And their girlfriends or wives never consider this a deficiency in character or motivation. Instead, they usually accept it as an inevitable genetic trait among males. Not surprisingly, this tolerance is more than welcomed by guys. Yet if asked why they can't boil water or simply locate their stove, men will often say, "I'm too busy to cook," or "My wife is better at it," or "I'm not allowed," or "I'd rather eat out."

Excuses, to be certain. But these morons are missing a grand opportunity, one that often eludes the accidental adult. That is, the opportunity to be viewed by friends and family as a thoughtful provider . . . a creative caretaker . . . a hero. By taking the time to prepare a meal for you and your loved ones, you are producing a tangible, satisfying (albeit consumable) product that clearly demonstrates your consideration for others. You also get to wield razor-sharp utensils, which is pretty cool. In the process of preparing a meal, you elevate yourself from the pack because you don't just bring home the bacon. No, you gently prepare it under a bubbling, buttery white wine sauce in a sauté pan along with some finely sliced shallots and porcini mushrooms. Yes, a man who cooks is a sophisticated, considerate, unexpected hero. And if there's anything an accidental adult loves, it's recognition for exceeding society's low expectations of himself and his ilk.

Need another benefit to pursuing the culinary arts? I've been married far too long for this perk to make much of a difference to me, but its advantages are undeniable. Simply put, women love men who can serve up a spicy homemade meal. They find them charming, attractive, and sensitive (which I'm told can sometimes lead to dessert for the chef). And what do women think about the guy whose hobby is, say . . . hunting? *Thanks for abandoning me for a weekend of drinking with the guys, playing with guns, and watching porn in your buddies' hunting shack!* The guy who plays fantasy football? *Is this why we took out a loan? For a twenty-four-hour sports entertainment cable package upgrade?* And the grown man whose favorite pastime is losing all concept of time while engaged in role-playing warfare video games? *Get out of the basement and grow up you jackass! Your kids need a daddy!*

Yes, the man who becomes a kitchen magician breaks the mold, impresses others, and fulfills a basic human need. So why don't I cook more often? Read on.

MATERIALS NEEDED

An uncluttered kitchen counter space free of children's bacteria-infested lunch bags, finger-stained homework assignments, and mud-soaked backpacks. In other words, the peaceful absence of kids underfoot. Unfortunately for many, a sanitary child-free work zone just isn't possible. Which is why I've largely placed cooking on the back burner and reserved it as a future hobby for when I'm an empty-nester or retired. This procrastination perfectly fits the accidental adult's lifestyle and philosophy: *I may be an adult aberration now, but I intend to become more skilled and constructive later in life. Just you wait!*

NECESSARY SKILLS

The ability to follow a recipe. This sometimes means distinguishing a difference between seemingly interchangeable directions like chop, dice, blanch, purée, and julienne. Unfortunately, following a recipe also usually requires math skills (Damn math! It's everywhere!) Sure, cups-to-quarts and pints-to-gallons conversion charts are always available, but it doesn't help that the abbreviations for teaspoon (tsp) and tablespoon (tbs) are practically identical to the impatient and easily distracted accidental adult.

TIME REQUIRED

When I was a kid, I used to help my mom bake cookies and cakes for our family nearly every weekend. By my teenage years, I had graduated to preparing some more significant family meals. This led me to conclude that practically every single recipe requires baking at 350°F for one hour. Then came college, and I started drinking. I quickly learned that meal readiness is measured neither by time nor temperature but instead by volume. The volume of alcohol consumed that is. For example: a strip steak on the grill, medium rare? One beer. Tacos with all the side dishes? Dos cervezas! A turkey dinner and all the trimmings? At least a half bottle of wine, if I can pry it from Kelly's hands.

BEFORE BEGINNING, ASK YOURSELF ...

"Am I secure with my sexuality?"

DON'T BE SURPRISED IF ...

Friends wonder if you're gay. That's okay, though. Even the coolest heterosexual guys who cook occasionally have to battle this ignorant and unfounded stereotype.

A few years ago, my friends and I went to see *The Bourne Identity* for our monthly Guys' Movie Night. In one memorable scene, super spy Jason Bourne is suffering amnesia, and he visits his apartment, which is now unfamiliar to him. As he tours his bachelor pad, trying to find a hint as to his pre-amnesia identity, he walks into his super-stylish, immaculate kitchen styled with the most chic décor, replete with shimmering stainless-steel gourmet cookware suspended with perfection from a ceiling rack. At this point, some wise-ass in the theater whispered a little too loudly (as if he were reading Bourne's mind), "Oh no! I'm gay!" Okay, so that wise-ass was me. But the point is, if super stud Jason Bourne can kick some serious spy ass, score with the ladies, *and* own one seriously tricked-out gourmet kitchen, then sign me up for cooking lessons. Quite the hetero hero, I'd say.

BE SURE TO TELL PEOPLE ...

"Of course I cook with an apron! It says 'KISS the cook' with the logo of my favorite face-painting hard rock band."

INWARD BOUND

My generation is known for its impatience, so it shouldn't surprise you that more than a few of my high school classmates already had retirement plans to share at our reunion: buy up a few acres in the country (the seniors' suburbs), maybe acquire a hobby farm, or build a cute little cabin on the lake.

Since I can't imagine ever launching a boat without jackknifing the trailer in front of an increasingly impatient assembly of aghast onlookers or waiting uncomfortably close in a line of half-naked men to use a public campground showerhouse, my future plans are obviously a tad less rustic. Unless I'm beachside under sunny skies, a life lived alfresco just isn't in the cards for me. Instead, if the fates (finances) will allow, Kelly and I plan on living in a downtown, upscale condo within an easy walking distance of theaters, rooftop bars, fun restaurants, bookstores, and entertainment centers. No weeds to pull, no lawn to mow, no trees to trim—just an outdoor patio balcony overlooking an urban skyline. Maybe a potted ivy snaking down the railing for kicks. I'll even take a riverfront or lakeview unit if one's available. To pass the time, who knows what hobbies or interests I'll have cultivated by then, though I'm certain it won't include Texas Hold 'em, ballroom dancing, or managing fantasy sports teams. In the spirit of most accidental adults, nine times out of ten I'll choose to live a reality that goes slightly against the grain of most typical adult expectations because that's the existence that feels right for me.

I understand our future plans aren't a good fit for many of my former classmates or today's neighbors and friends (hearty souls that they are). But that's okay. It's our retirement, not theirs. And at the rate we're underfunding it, that day may never come anyway.

So while I spend my free time enjoying the great indoors as I write, play music, and relish a few great days of running in the sun (when the weather holds), I understand many of my nature-loving friends might remain puzzled by my choice of recreations. But coming from the guy whose former high school classmates labeled "The Least Changed," my hobbies really shouldn't surprise them. All I ask from the real adults is the same respect they'd show a walleye. Let me off the hook. Gently, please.

f us never planned o
his happening. But it di
ometime between gra
chool and our first mort
age, a strange phenom
non began replacing ou
outhful mojos with
ew-found maturity. Ar
e didn't see it comin
ur two-door coupe
orphed into sliding
oor minivans. Bar-hop
ing turned into mov
ights on the couch. No
e write letters to th
ditor. And golf? It's

12. NOSTALGIA

Checking In with Your Inner Child

LIKE MOST TEENAGERS, I THOUGHT many of my high school teachers sounded a bit like the teacher Miss Othmar from those Charlie Brown television specials—issuing indistinguishable trombone-like *mwa-mwa-wah* noises where helpful, meaningful, and instructional phrases should exist.

Then there was my savior, Miss Kalfahs, or Keri, as I preferred to call her (mentally, that is, at least until after graduation). Barely into her midtwenties, Miss Kalfahs arrived on the scene in my Midwestern Catholic high school to take her place as a fresh-faced unmarried English teacher cast among a handful of sisters, brothers, and priests on the faculty who didn't quite know what to make of her. But I did. To me, she was a hero who awakened my appreciation for the written word by giving us creative assignments like writing letters to David Letterman, with an A+ promised to anyone whose letter got read on his show. She encouraged colorful, content-appropriate dialogue in our writing—even if it included mature

"A blanket of snow covered my nude body."

—Colin Sokolowski, age seventeen, English Composition Honors

themes and mild profanity (hell yeah!). Outside of class, Miss Kalfahs treated us like the adults we weren't with candid stories from her brief first marriage and with provocative tales from her days as the girlfriend of a security guard who sneaked her backstage at rock 'n' roll concerts to witness debauchery unlike anything we'd ever hope to see ourselves.

And it didn't hurt that she was kind of hot.

Yes, I was smitten. But it wasn't so much a case of "hot for teacher" as it was "in awe of teacher." Never before and never since did I have a teacher who encouraged me to explore honest emotions and express them in writing without fear of ridicule or judgment. With Miss Kalfahs as a mentor, I grew comfortable liberating a writing style that felt natural and honest to me—a voice that became uniquely my own.

Too bad it was such a stunted voice.

ENGLISH COMPOSITION (HONORS, OF COURSE)

Schools are often breeding grounds for great literary talent. One of my favorite authors proves this. About 100 years ago, F. Scott Fitzgerald was publishing smart literary works for the newspaper at his prep school in St. Paul. Yes, at the ripe age of thirteen, the future Great American Novelist wrote intriguing stories like the detective tale "The Mystery of the Raymond Mortgage," which students at his school still read and review to this day.

Then there was me.

Like the young Jazz Age author, I too was churning out volumes of essays and short stories as a teenager. Scotty and I were kindred spirits. We both touched on themes of despair, youth, and promise. Except at the age of seventeen, I was writing essays comparing

Shakespeare's use of mistaken identity and sexual innuendo with
story lines from the sitcom *Three's Company*:

> *Most of the sexual references used on* Three's Company *are never
> as discreet as in Shakespeare's works. Looking intently over Bill's
> works, you will eventually discover an innuendo, but in watch-
> ing* Three's Company *you never have to watch too long before
> you'll be morally offended.*

Other times I was penning God-awful poetry fantasizing about
a future escape from my claustrophobic small town in search of a
bigger city in which:

> *The night comes slowly
> but never leaves.
> As if to say
> "Live in me, and I will bring you
> HAPPINESS!"
> With blue lights glowing over the skyline
> and that saxophone
> that dances in your mind.*

For one assignment, I even found myself drafting brief, sexually
obtuse metaphors with seasonal themes:

> *1. The leaves were a whirlwind of browns and yellows blowing
> across my exposed lower body.*

> *2. Skiing topless, her temperature was a ringing alarm clock.*

> *3. My neighbor's wife was a cinder of passion in the snowbank.*

(For which I earned a full twenty out of twenty points along with a red-inked, "A bit too erotic, Colin!" admonition from Miss Kalfahs. Not bad!)

I'd even use class time to write stream-of-consciousness "tales from home" and mail them to my beloved older sister Megan who was away at college:

> *I'm ordering a pink shirt out of the Lands' End catalog, even though it's $18, but I'm using my B. Dalton money that I won because we were second in sales for the 1985 Holiday Season and it's worth the money because I really need one, and I know it will be good quality. . . . Those bastards at Musicland never got any more Walkman players in yet even though they said to check back today, and when I checked back today she said to check back on Friday. . . . I got asked to the Turnabout dance by Heidi Hansen and I offered to drive so it'll be easier on her 'cause she's a Frosh. She's really fun to be with, and she just might even be better looking than her sister, and she smells good too. . . . Is there any way I can get my Police calendar back?*

Any kind of writing was time well spent, according to Miss Kalfahs, who understood that few if any of her students (myself included) would ever become literary giants like the young Fitzgerald. On most days, she'd simply settle for correct spelling, proper grammar, and legible penmanship from her pupils. More often than not, my writing was far from intellectual. It was mostly intended to provide comic relief for my classmates and ultimately to impress my muse, Miss Kalfahs. But whatever the reason for my smart-ass prose, I must have felt some sense of pride in my high school writing, because after all these years I've kept many of my essays, poems, and book reports, jammed inside a tattered green Trapper Portfolio folder, never predicting that decades later I would get a chance to dig out those dog-eared pages and re-examine my juvenile psyche—in front of a crowded bar.

REDEMPTION THROUGH HUMILIATION

In case you're wondering, there actually is a word for some of the crap you wrote when you were a kid. *Juvenilia* is a centuries-old term that describes the early literary, musical, or other creative works of a young artist. In most cases, calling a sophomore-year off-color haiku a literary work is something of a stretch. But today, poetry-slam organizers, open-mic night hosts, and even some websites have broadened that term (largely for comedic effect) to encompass much more.

Remember that letter you wrote to your girlfriend, apologizing for flirting with the new freshman girl in the cafeteria and begging her to take you back so you can go to Homecoming because your dad is giving you the keys to the Oldsmobile station wagon along with an extended curfew to 11 P.M.? Well, that's juvenilia. Remember that rap you wrote to the beat of DJ Jazzy Jeff & the Fresh Prince's "Parents Just Don't Understand," chastising your mom and dad for grounding you after you "forgot" that 11 P.M. curfew? That's juvenilia. And remember that diary entry you wrote promising the world you'd someday become more famous than Huey Lewis (or the News) and you'd tour the world with your band finally free of your parents' lame-ass 11 P.M. curfew? That's also juvenilia. And for accidental adults, it's comedy gold.

If by some stroke of good fortune you've happened to hang onto old diaries, or eighth-grade movie scripts, or letters returned by scorned sweethearts, for God's sake don't hide them in a shoebox under your dresser. That sappy shit deserves to be laughed at by others. Believe it or not, literary organizations, bar owners, website publishers, and a host of other sadistic groups are hosting juvenilia events everywhere, offering what one group calls "personal redemption through public humiliation." In other words, adults are encouraged to share their shame by exposing their pubescent perspectives on life, love, and homemade Air Supply–style song lyrics for the empathetic enjoyment of a live audience who feels their pain—mainly because they wrote garbage like that, too. In return, accidental adults get to grab a microphone and reconnect with their younger, cooler, and goofier sides. A win-win for all.

My first experience with one of these juvenilia events transpired within a cozy room called the Titanic Lounge inside a favorite Minneapolis bar, Kieran's Irish Pub. And it proved almost as cathartic as it was entertaining.

OPEN MIC, CLOSED MODESTY

"How will I know if they're laughing with me or if they're laughing at me?" I nervously asked Kelly as we drove downtown to meet our friends at the bar.

"What's the difference, as long as they laugh?" she rationalized.

Great. So I'll be baring a part of my soul for a few cheap laughs, many of which will be at my expense? At least I won't be alone on the sacrificial altar of comedy, I trusted.

And I was right. About a dozen other masochists registered to read their writings along with me. Kelly was right, too. The readers didn't seem to mind if the audience was laughing with them or at them. Fortunately for the audience, the performers seemed to care more about sharing their juvenile writings than protecting their adult egos. And their work truly was juvenile.

First there was the somewhat nerdy middle-aged man who read an essay he wrote in junior high after discovering his cable company had temporarily unscrambled the signal to HBO, giving him a free weekend of televised nudity, violence, and adult language. His hilarious essay revealed in embarrassing detail the preteen fantasy he developed after watching the shower scene of a 1983 thriller featuring a very soapy Catherine Deneuve who starred as a 4,000-year-old Egyptian vampire.

Then came the twentysomething woman who shared a high school poem for which she compiled a lengthy list of all the things that frightened her. For the next five minutes, she read that catalog of neuroses, ranging from "I'm scared of losing my virginity" to "I'm scared of keeping my virginity" to "I'm scared of not being able to sleep" to "I'm scared of not being able to wake up." At the merciful conclusion, she explained (to no one's surprise) that when her mother accidentally discovered the poem, it prompted her to schedule an appointment for her daughter with a psychiatrist, STAT.

After a few more awkward works of angsty adolescent art, it was finally my turn.

If I'm going to do this, I may as well fully commit, I thought. So to really get into the spirit of the event, I snapped on my high school letter jacket, which proved to be only *slightly* tight in the midsection (thankyouverymuch). If my essay wouldn't reveal enough about its uncool author, my jacket certainly would, decorated with a silver medal for a second place finish in a tennis tournament, a shiny gold Student Council four-year service pin (a real chick magnet), and a brass pin that simply says BAND ('nuff said, right?).

After self-medicating with two pints of Harp, I had mustered all the courage I needed to read an essay I had written in my senior year of high school that would essentially declare to a room full of adult strangers that I was a teenage chauvinist pig. Wearing that bitchin' jacket, I offered a short introduction explaining how this essay was tragically inspired by a failed date during which I spent $14 for a steak dinner for two at Ponderosa and received in return no payoff at the end of the night. Then I recited my astonishingly misguided take on reverse gender discrimination, my masterpiece. . . .

"It's Not My World; It's a Woman's World"

You may find it surprising to believe that from my point of view, the female gender is discriminatory. It usually goes the other way; men discriminate against women. But in my world, the women rule.

At my place of employment as a bookstore clerk, I am the only male employee. I am also the only employee who sweeps, takes out the cardboard, takes out the garbage, and is volunteered by the manager for putting up Northway Mall Christmas decorations. Coincidence or discrimination?

Don't get me wrong. I do enjoy my job. The new skills I've learned such as dusting books and vacuuming will help me as I go throughout life with liberated female managers.

When it comes to relationships, it is clearly evident who is in charge. It is the female who determines how often they will see each other, what they will do, and how much money should be spent on her. If you don't believe me, watch a young couple who's out on a date. If the lady so much as mentions she'd like to sit in the car and "talk," the male is reduced to a blob of JELL-O forcing out the words, "OOOOhhh Kayyy." It is also the female who will decide if they will actually talk or not.

Watching a guy getting yelled at by his girlfriend is very unnerving. A normally loud, dominant male can be reduced to the size of a mouse. Guys will do anything to keep their girlfriends happy.

I understand that "Sokolowski" is not the most attractive name in the world. There are several supposedly modern women in the world who will keep their maiden names 'til death! I believe in true equality, and all due rights for women, but if my future bride will not accept my last name as hers, then I'll have to end our relationship. Yes, that's right. I'll quit my job.

Feeling ten pounds lighter, I thanked the audience for listening and returned to my table, immediately grabbing my beer and looking for some feedback on my performance.

"What did you think?" I asked my friend Chuck.

"My head hurts from laughing," he said.

Not convinced that was a good sign, I turned to Kelly and asked, "So were they all laughing with me or at me?"

"Are you going to finish your fries?" was her loving response.

STAYING AFLOAT

Ironically in the Titanic Lounge that night, the readers' spirits actually seemed buoyed by the audience's support, despite the shared tales of high school heartbreak and countless social setbacks. Each of us seemed to learn the same lesson that night: Give an audience an evening of brutally honest and awkwardly hysterical entertainment, and they will sound their approval. And if you think about it, I suppose it makes perfect sense. In sharing their juvenile compositions with a roomful of strangers, the participants were giving the audience permission to laugh at their twisted, adolescent rantings. And in return, the audience could choose either to laugh with them or at them. That unique mixture of self-deprecation and commiseration is not only a beautiful combination, it's quite possibly the recipe for a perfect accidental adult society.

See, most accidental adults have long ago discovered that laughing at their precarious roles in this super-serious adult world is always more fun than crying. And knowing you're not alone in your disinclined journey to adulthood is critical to your sanity and ultimate survival. So for reluctant grownups everywhere, forget *The Catcher in the Rye*. Juvenilia is required reading.

So why not indulge in a bit of juvenilia from time to time? What's that, you say? Communal disgrace just isn't your thing? I can completely understand you might be reluctant to intentionally humiliate yourself in public (despite your occasional unintentional success in this endeavor). But before you can object further, I've got three easy steps to get you moving in the right direction—along the road to recovery.

THREE-STEP PROGRAM FOR JUVENILES IN RECOVERY

Maybe it's a video of you wearing a coconut bra and a grass skirt from your junior year performance in *South Pacific*. Maybe it's an audio tape of the night you actually got through to speak to Phil Collins on the national radio program "Rockline." Maybe it's the drawing you did for your summer girlfriend that recreated the *Pretty in Pink* poster with your face in place of Duckie's alongside Molly Ringwald's and Andrew McCarthy's characters. Whatever possession you have that triggers memories of your childhood and allows you to reconnect you with your inner child—well, finding that treasure is a lot like striking oil. And it's time to drill!

STEP 1. REPO YOUR CRAP

If you haven't cleared out all of your old junk from your parents'
house, then snap to it the next time you visit home. If you're like me
and your crap now sits strewn across the floor of your own basement, take a minute to weed through those shoeboxes of childhood
memories in hopes of finding something worth a laugh. You might
find a sweat-stained copy of your old student council presidential
election speech in which you suggested your opponent may not be
fit for office because she was too academically gifted and needed to
take a few chill pills (whereas your platform promised your school
nine months of wicked fun and some totally tight DJ dances every
month). Maybe you'll find your rambling seven-page book report on
"How setting affects the characters in *Wuthering Heights*"—a classic
novel you still haven't read yet. At the very least, you might ironically discover you've officially forgotten about the jerk who wrote
in your yearbook, "Forget the books, forget the class, forget me and
I'll kick your ass!"

STEP 2. CELEBRATE YOUR PROGRESS

If you're lucky enough to unearth an old letter, video or painting,
sit back, dig in, and enjoy the moment. It may be more therapeutic to
share your nostalgic memento with others as juvenilia event-goers
have found, but there's nothing wrong with simply keeping it to
yourself either. In today's solemn and super sober world, accidental
and assimilated adults alike deserve to check out from time to time,
and check in with their inner-child. Especially when reconnecting
with your childhood illustrates just how far you've actually come—
a boost any accidental adult can appreciate. Sure, you may still be

that jackass who gives his buddy a check for his wedding written for exactly $102.67, and then adds "good drugs" on the memo line. But at least you've graduated beyond guilt-writing to your older sister from college, "I'll give you your birthday present when I come home next. In the meantime, here's $20 of my work study money. I'll send more later."

STEP 3. SUPPORT YOUR PEERS

If a tour through old memorabilia doesn't produce any embarrassing essays, ridiculous radio plays, or cheesy homemade videos, then at least live vicariously through others by attending a juvenilia event near you. It may be part of a local poetry slam or some bar's open mic night. Wherever you can find one, pull up a barstool and enjoy the show. No luck finding an event? Create your own, and assure your participating guests that their audience will be kind. Just remember that misery loves company. Your presence alone should tell others, "I'm laughing with you, not at you"—unless the readers are as insecure as I am. Then whose problem is that?

GIVE THANKS FOR THE ANGST

Quite out of the blue, Miss Kalfahs looked me up and sent me a "Let's catch up" e-mail some years ago, and we've been trading messages ever since. I had actually planned on tracking her down eventually to share some of my writing with her, to show her the monster she helped create. But truth be told, I'm flattered she found me first. She had hundreds of students and scores of essays to read and grade over the years, but this wannabe Fitzgerald had only one Zelda to impress with his writing, and I'm glad my impression was a lasting one.

But I'm not disillusioned. I fully realize the Midwestern high school that Miss Kalfahs and I left many years ago won't add my book to their collections, sandwiched between *The Great Gatsby* and *Tender Is the Night*. And I'm certain the English Comp. teachers there won't ever ask their classes to dissect and discuss my juvenilia like the St. Paul Academy instructors require their students to analyze Fitzgerald's earliest works. (Although I've got a stuffed Trapper Keeper I'd be happy to lend you guys if you decide. Call me!)

Likewise, I will never be disappointed should I be excluded from those bookshelves that feature the world's most esteemed works. Instead, I've discovered that it doesn't take the Great American Novel to stir a reader's soul. Sometimes even the most juvenile juvenilia can touch a person's deepest emotions or strike a resounding chord with everyday people—even if it's unintentional.

Ever since I shared my juvenilia with a bar full of strangers, I've realized that high school students actually have a lot in common with us accidental adults. As teenagers sit in English classes, churning out overly dramatic essays about their struggle to fit into the outside world, accidental adults like us stare out the windows of our offices and wonder where our place is in this overly serious adultcentric world.

To accidental adults everywhere, I offer you two simple wishes. The first is that someday, like me, you too can discover and hold onto a lasting, creative outlet to express your tales of angst—a platform for sharing mortifying experiences and revealing your inner juvenile in an unashamed voice with a seemingly empathetic audience.

My second wish is that you find that crap you wrote back in school and share it so someday complete strangers like me can laugh their asses off when we hear it.

Remember . . . we're laughing with you, not at you . . . (as far as you know).

us never planned o
is happening. But it di
ometime between gra
chool and our first mort
age, a strange phenom
non began replacing ou
outhful mojos with
ew-found maturity. An
e didn't see it coming
ur two-door coupe
orphed into sliding
oor minivans. Bar-hop
ng turned into movi
ghts on the couch. No
e write letters to th
itor. And golfs. It's n

CONCLUSION

Let's Stick Together

SO WHAT HAVE WE LEARNED? After twelve chapters of foible-filled anecdotes peppered with capricious advice, I'd understand if by now you've concluded that I'm something of an incompetent, flippant smartass. I had that coming.

"This taught me a lesson, but I'm not quite sure what it is."

—John McEnroe

Instead, I'd be thrilled if the pages of this book helped you discover that you actually have something in common with this smartass: a shared membership in the accidental adult club. Even better? I'd love to imagine you now possess the tools necessary to develop your own set of coping skills for those times when the world of assimilated adults comes crashing down upon you. And it will. Believe me, it will.

Not sure if you're prepared to sit at the adult table just yet? Sure you are. But just to be safe, let's re-examine a few tricks of the trade and review some of the fundamental philosophies you'll need in order to avoid banishment to life's kiddie card table in the corner.

Embrace Your Inner Smart-Ass and Fuel Your
Inner Monologue

If you glean nothing else from these pages, this is the ultimate lesson to master. Why? A sardonic and sarcastic silent conversation with yourself not only provides an outlet for your adulthood angst, it keeps you company when you feel alone and outnumbered. Keeping irreverence to yourself also shelters your stunted maturity from any unnecessary exposure. When a coworker earnestly admits, "I hope the stimulus package works fast," your unspoken "That's what she said!" monologue proves no one enjoys that inadvertent innuendo more than you. And really, isn't amusing yourself the point anyway?

Feign Interest in (and Familiarity with)
Adult Endeavors

It's disappointing to admit this, but sometimes you simply have to go along to get along. So fake it when necessary, but apply this principle sparingly. Overuse can lead to prolonged exposure to adult conversations from which you'll learn useless nuggets like how to improve your credit score or where to find the freshest organic produce this side of the Mississippi River—just because you nodded, squinted contemplatively, and appeared convincing when you said you've always wanted to know . . . .

Lighten Up!

Ferris Bueller's approach to life shouldn't be dismissed as a thing of our youth. What's wrong with embracing it today? Checking in with our inner adolescent reconnects us to a wonderful, carefree, and thrilling spirit that nourishes our soul. It's a beautiful thing to throw a little caution to the wind, act young at heart, and play hooky from life every now and then—so long as you know when it's time to check out of that addictive yet unsustainable mindset and rejoin the grownup world again. So let's take the Ferris Bueller philosophy and apply it to our adult lives whenever life gets too serious, complicated, or demanding. How can we possibly be expected to handle life/work/parenting/home improvements on a day like this? The school-skipping, life-living character in the film put it best when he observed, "Life moves pretty fast. You don't stop and look around once in a while, you could miss it." Pretty smart for a kid.

Cultivate Company

Your version of Guyhood will likely look different than mine, and that's okay. All that matters is that you assemble and nurture a group of like-minded friends who are similarly stunted accidental adults. This way, you'll never truly feel alone. Unless you're looking for company at a wine-tasting party. Then you're probably on your own.

Don't Confuse Ignorance with Incompetence

Try this exercise: Make a list of all the things you can't do but society says you probably ought to know by now. (If you're like me, you might want to use legal-sized paper. Narrow ruled.) Now go back to that list and circle all the items that you really care to learn. Not many circles are there? So why would you beat yourself up over your lack of understanding about things of no interest or importance to you?

Never confuse not knowing with an inability to learn. If you cared enough about a particular adult topic or activity, you'd learn about it. Hell, you might even master it. You learned the best way to prevent an audit is to pay a professional to prepare your taxes for you, didn't you? Now don't be surprised at the skills or expertise you pick up inadvertently along the way. Which brings us to . . .

Expect Evolutions

So you're pretty sure you now understand the difference between rotating your tires and balancing your tires. Some would call this progress. Die-hard accidental adults might consider it selling out. I simply call it inevitable. Don't worry. A slight metamorphosis of maturity doesn't mean you've become "one of them." Chances are, your journey as a reluctant grownup will feature plenty of relapses, ensuring your membership in the accidental adulthood society is not in jeopardy of revocation anytime soon. Need evidence? Once a week without fail, aren't you still that well-intentioned but absent-minded homeowner who drags his garbage cans to the curb, walks back to the garage, gets into his vehicle, and backs out of the driveway smacking into the cans, having forgotten the previous thirty seconds of his life? When you're angry with your spouse, you're still the guy who grabs his kids' Speak & Spell toy keyboard and repeatedly presses the F and U buttons in rapid succession, aren't you? You still unplug most electrical cords by sharply yanking on them several feet away from the outlet, don't you? When a neighbor drives by while you're watering the plants outside, you still lewdly wag the garden hose between your legs while waving to her, right? And if you luck into snagging a particularly convenient parking space in a crowded lot, you usually still shout, "Rock star parking!" like you did in high school, right? Thought so.

Stick Together

Some days, living among super-serious, responsible adults can make you want to go to your garage, close the door, and turn on the car. But allow me to suggest a considerably less dramatic approach that can lead to coexistence. First realize that try as we might, we simply can't change these assimilated adults. It's their world, and we're just squatters hoping no one will notice our flawed but proud existence (and praying they won't force us to cough up the rent in the currency of conformity, because that's one hell of a price to pay). So instead of fighting them, why not channel our contempt for convention and stick together as unified accidental adults? This not only sounds good in theory, but in practice it actually requires very little effort.

When we see the guy in his driveway swearing at his silent snow blower because he seized his single-stage engine by mistakenly filling the gas tank with a two-cycle oil and gas mixture, let's admit to him that we made that same $500 mistake not too long ago ourselves. When we see a neighbor using a blunt hatchet to cut down a tree that summarily falls on top of him as if to say "Serves you right, you nature-hating bastard!" let's bring him a beer and some bandages (before asking him for some firewood). When we see a guy hoist his frothy pint of Budweiser during a champagne toast at a classy black-tie event . . . well, let's give that kindred spirit a collective hug. Full frontal, of course.

ONE FOR ALL, ALL FOR ONE

As we live the carefree lives of accidental adults, we should expect the indignant adult world is going to pull the curtain on us from time to time. At moments like these, I hope you'll channel your inner ambivalence and discover there's a richness to be found as a member of an empathetic (and apathetic) community bound together in kinship through shared dismissiveness. If you do, you'll likely realize that going through life with a penchant for blunders isn't so bad as long as you're equipped with a detached indifference fueled by the sweet realization that you don't walk the path alone.

If we can stick together, accidental adulthood truly can be a satisfying, grand way of life. But like all good things, it too is temporary. So enjoy it while you can. Before you know it, you'll find yourself lingering on the Hallmark Channel just a little longer than you should during a night of aimless channel surfing. And soon you'll think the music inside Abercrombie & Fitch is annoyingly loud, and you'll be royally pissed when their sales associates call you "sir." Yes, like it or not, eventually we all grow up. Even accidental adults like me.

BETTER LATE THAN NEVER

One of my longest-held dreams began in high school, when my friend Louie and I fantasized that we were someday going to become published authors. Along the way, we'd rent a rundown New York City apartment. We'd eat cold ravioli right out of the can and drink warm Old Milwaukee. We'd be piss poor. And we'd be happy.

Decades later, both of us have forged different careers in different cities. We earn enough money to eat well-balanced meals. And I'd say we're both reasonably happy with our lives. But neither of us has given up on that dream to someday become a published author.

As I conclude this work, I'm reminded of that high school dream, and I have to think . . . better late than never. Sharing these pent-up tales and tips with you has proven cathartic beyond my wildest dreams. And to think that this book might help some readers navigate the road to reluctant adulthood and take comfort in knowing there are other accidental adults out there? Ironically, that makes me feel downright "adult."

If it's true that writing a book is in fact adultlike, to that I say so be it. Because adulthood, in and of itself, is not to be feared so long as growing old doesn't mean growing up. And I don't think I'm in danger of completely growing up any time soon.

The years will inevitably push all of us to adulthood. When this happens, remember that adulthood really isn't a destination. It's a journey. And if you maintain the right attitude, sometimes the best journeys you will ever take in life will come about by accident.

— — —

Good talk, Rusty. Good talk.

Photo by Greg Helgeson

ABOUT THE AUTHOR

Who is The Accidental Adult?

COLIN SOKOLOWSKI is the guy friends call to answer music trivia questions, not for help hanging Sheetrock. He also can't tell the difference between a Chianti or a Cabernet and he really doesn't care. When he's playing the part of a grownup, Colin is a communications professional in the field of education and has written a variety of articles for Twin Cities media. He and his wife live in St. Paul, Minnesota, where he gives scooter rides to their three children. He invites you to read about his reluctant journey into adulthood at *www.accidentaladult.com*.